CULTIVATING A BELIEF SYSTEM FOR PEACE, EQUITY AND SOCIAL JUSTICE FOR ALL

JOSEPH NWOYE

CULTIVATING A BELIEF SYSTEM FOR PEACE, EQUITY AND SOCIAL JUSTICE FOR ALL

iUniverse books may be ordered through booksellers or by contacting:

iUniverse
1663 Liberty Drive
Bloomington, IN 47403
www.iuniverse.com
1-800-Authors (1-800-288-4677)

ISBN: 978-1-5320-7273-4 (sc)
ISBN: 978-1-5320-7274-1 (e)

Library of Congress Control Number: 2019906251

Print information available on the last page.

iUniverse rev. date: 06/10/2019

Contents

PART 1
THE BELIEF SYSTEM AND SUBSEQUENT
TRANSFORMATION ON ISSUES TO FOSTER
EQUITY AND SOCIAL JUSTICE

PART 2
INTERNATIONAL BELIEF SYSTEM

CULTURAL FRAMING IN BELIEF FORMATION: UNDERSTANDING CULTURAL DIFFERENCES IN SHAPING DIFFERENTIAL HUMAN BEHAVIORS

PART 3
EDUCATIONAL ISSUES AND THE NEED FOR BELIEF TRANSFORMATION

Inspiration for the Book

This book was conceived based upon the numerous experiences I have had with diverse groups of people over the years. Most of my experiences are a direct result of my extroverted personality, beginning with my very close family of ten: Mom, Dad, and eight children—four boys and four girls. As a result of the closeness I experienced in my family and the people in my neighborhood, I began my life with the belief that all humans are by nature good. I learned how to communicate effectively with anyone, from any country in Africa, Asia, South America, Europe, and North America, particularly the United States, regardless of whether they are black or white, male or female, or their sexual orientation.

Through collaborative engagement with other people, I made great friends; friends who have trusted and confided in me, and in return, I have trusted and confided in them. For me, it was an exciting time, a time when I was drawn to people with whom I engaged in meaningful exploration of our varied experiences. Of course, I learned a lot and gained experience from all those I crossed paths with. We did a lot together; it was the best of times.

In my earlier days after traveling abroad, especially when I entered college, it was not easy for me to make close friends. This was due in part from the cultural shock of moving from a place where everyone spoke to each other to a place where people only spoke to the people they knew.

At times, I would meet people who, even though I would speak with them at a deeper level, I ended up questioning their character. One such incident occurred in 1985, during my sophomore year at Indiana University of Pennsylvania. I had an experience that remains very vivid in my memory and probably will remain until I die. A student I will call "John" asked me, "Is it true that there are people who live in the trees and caves in Africa?" I began to question myself: "Do we really have people who are so ignorant about others that they could ask such unexpected and condescending questions?" John was not unintelligent or racist; he was just someone who could not do the basic research to inform himself on primary issues before asking questions.

John was a sophomore in college; the company he kept throughout his formative years had mis-educated him about Africa and how the people live. I believe that the experience with people (such as myself) who were different from those he grew up with helped put John at ease and fostered his quest to know more about people from various parts of the world. John aside, there were other people that stood out; people you instantaneously knew were driven by a genuine and burning desire to learn. They asked questions that others did not want to ask, questions that might sound inappropriate for some, but reflected their true and authentic understanding of issues based on what they were taught, and that provided a unique forum for more meaningful learning.

This and similar incidences have planted the seed for the journey that I have undertaken; and I still remain steadfast in my core belief that people are by-and-large good. In writing this book, I intend to reassure apprehensive individuals that there is nothing to fear from people who are not like them or those who do not fit into their ideological orbit based on their cultural upbringing or the company they keep. Rather, I encourage apprehensive individuals to focus their attentions and efforts on knowing and understanding those who are different from them. It is my contention that those who may at first glance appear different are in fact the people these apprehensive individuals will learn the most from. Believe me, I learned the most from people like John.

As I left Indiana University of Pennsylvania to teach at West Liberty University in West Liberty, West Virginia, I felt that I was on a mission. I was on my way to change the world. I am convinced, more than ever, that people from different cultures (especially now that the winds of globalization are blowing around the world), continuously see racist-driven behaviors for what they are – ignorance. Unfortunately, very few want to discuss these issues or the artificial walls that consistently cultivate and develop the concept of "us versus them." We live in a culture that continues to divide people on the basis of their race and ethnicity, and yet people have conveniently swept these problems under the rug, as if they are not part of our experience and who we are. I hope that this book will prompt the desired debate and discussions as to why we have a misconception within our society (and globally), a misconception that impacts all of us and propels some to continuously engage in both overt and covert discriminatory practices that stem from how they were taught about people who are unlike them.

Again, the purpose of this book is to engage with all people within their varied cultures and backgrounds, to get to know them and study or learn why they act the way they do. I am interested and excited to engage all people in our quest to create a trusting space in which people of all races, ideation, and socioeconomic strata come together to help overcome cultural blind spots. You can better explain and predict the responses of others when you get to know them in meaningful ways; perhaps if you do, you too will understand what I have come to realize. Human beings are by nature good, and that we will realize the same if we are less judgmental.

Foreword

Christine Sleeter

California State University Monterey Bay

Cultivating a Belief System for Peace, Equity and Social Justice for All, a book of wisdom for any time, is especially timely now. The United States, one of the most diverse nations in the world, espouses in its Pledge of Allegiance, the enduring central value of liberty and justice for all. Yet, the U.S. still grapples with its ongoing legacy of slavery and theft of indigenous peoples' land, as well as with waves of immigrants searching for a better life. What do liberty and justice mean when millions of citizens, and thousands more immigrants, are of religious backgrounds other than Christian? What does it mean to uphold liberty and justice for the thousands of immigrants and refugees fleeing war, persecution, and poverty in various parts of the world, most of whom, unlike a century ago, do not come from Europe? What do our nation's central values mean when including newcomers or grappling with movements such as #BlackLivesMatter and #MeToo means changing how things have "always" been done?

In *Cultivating a Belief System for Peace, Equity and Social Justice for All,* Joseph Nwoye challenges us to reflect critically on beliefs we may hold about other people that contradict or undermine equity and justice. Where do our beliefs come from? How do they influence us, and of concern here, how do they lead us to act in ways that are unfair or discriminatory? Nwoye believes in the capacity of individuals to grow and change; none of us inherits a belief system that is immutable. But neither do we automatically inherit a sense of accountability for what we believe and do. **Laced with poignant examples, stories, and compassion,** *Cultivating a Belief System for Peace, Equity and Social Justice* **offers needed tools for examining what we believe, how our beliefs impact on our behavior, and how we might transform those beliefs in order to affirm liberty and justice for all of us.**

Acknowledgements

I have read the works of many authors, and by and large, they are in agreement that they could not have written their works without the support they received from their family, friends, editors, and colleagues. This book is no different; I could not have written this book or my other books alone. To that end, I would like to mention some of the people who directly or indirectly helped me on this journey. A friend and colleague characterized this book as "both an insightful and extremely relevant book for our times." It is based upon this that I gratefully and humbly thank the following...

First, I would like to begin by expressing my heartfelt gratitude and thanks to Dr. Mark DeHainaut and his wife Professor Kimberly DeHainaut for their painstaking and repeated reading through all the chapters and providing me with feedback that adds value to this book. Similarly, I would like to thank my friend, Dr. Wayne Benenson, with whom I have worked in various capacities over the years, from Illinois State University to present time. Big thanks also go to Professor Christine Sleeter, a distinguished professor whose speeches and writings helped develop the framework for my professional work, including writing this book; she has been a valuable resource. Thank you to the anonymous reviewer of this book as well as Dr. Godson Chukwuma, who also read parts of this book and engaged with me in various discussions about how our belief systems shape our behaviors.

I would also like to remember my friends, Drs. Edwina and Larry Vold, for providing me the window through which to understand the impact of economic inequity in determining success or failure of members of our society. Drs. Vold provided me with the foundational desire to study and understand the impact that discrimination from the past has had upon discriminatory practices found today in and outside academia and other workplaces. These discriminatory practices are reflected in the Department of Justices' reports documenting not one, but all three cities (Baltimore, Chicago, and Ferguson) they investigated for unfair treatment of certain segments of our society.

I would also want to extend my thanks to my students at Illinois State University and West Liberty College in Wheeling, West Virginia, especially to those who participated in the Urban Seminar – a program that helped to create a forum for aspiring suburban professional teachers to engage with urban children, in what can best be described as a dramatic program to bring people together while providing the aspiring suburban teachers with culturally responsive tools to teach all children, regardless of their race or social economic situation, the program was especially memorable and perhaps one of the best in the nation. I am proud to have had the opportunity to participate. The program also reminds me of my friend "Bruce." Bruce was a part of the urban program profile in Chapter 10 of this book. During that time, many participants committed to changing the world for the better, especially Bruce, whose life work and commitment to helping the vulnerable among us contributed to him giving his all, including giving his life to save others who were different from him. He was an exemplary advocate for children, may his gentle soul rest in peace.

Finally, I want to thank my supportive and precious wife, Melinda Nwoye, who consistently reminds me every day of the need to help those whose only obstacle to success is lack of opportunity and caring people in their lives. How could I forget my precious children Uchenna, Obianuju, and Chioma, my wonderful brothers and sisters, Amechi, Nnanyelugo, Chineze, Ngozi, and Nwakaego. They are my inspiration in all I do, and their unconditional love sustains me and motivates me in all I do. You are collectively the best family anyone could wish to have and I am certainly blessed to have you all as members of my family. I thank you from the deepest part of my heart and our common connection to the greatest and best parents anyone could ask for, my father Nkaonadi Emmanuel Okeke and my mother Onuoma Josephine Nwoye.

Thank you all with humility,

Joseph Nwoye.

PART 1

THE BELIEF SYSTEM AND SUBSEQUENT TRANSFORMATION ON ISSUES TO FOSTER EQUITY AND SOCIAL JUSTICE

CHAPTER 1

HISTORICAL DIMENSION TO AMERICA'S SEPARATE CULTURES

The word "immigrant" reminds us of who we are and where we came from. Except for Native Americans, we are all immigrants from different places with unique cultures, some of which over time we lose and others we maintain. Sometimes, we cannot influence change in some of the things that make us different from others, as in the case of our skin pigmentation. The extent to which we lose or retain our unique cultures determines the degree to which it influence one's engagement within the larger community. This phenomenon, to some extent, explains the relative historical and cultural divisions in our society. The degree to which one loses or retains his or her culture is a function of controllable and uncontrollable factors and the degree to which one is integrated into the community. In general, these controllable and uncontrollable factors significantly explain the divisions that are apparent in our society, the divisions that some people deny and that others pretend do not exist. To overcome these apparent divisions, we must first accept the fact that they do exist. Denial or pretending that they do not exist will not remedy the situation. We must be united in accepting that there are divisions and work towards a resolution that can only be achieved by confronting the factors that contributed to the creation of these divisions in the first place.

President Abraham Lincoln reminds us that "A house divided against itself cannot stand." Despite President Lincoln's powerful reminder, we are still a house divided. The reasons for these divisions are based on our history, geography, cultural upbringing, racial differences, religious upbringing, political stands, and nationality affiliations etc. In this chapter, we will explore the factors that have and continue to influence the divisions in our society. For example, in an article titled "What is nationalism? Its history and what it means in 2018," Ann Sraders asserts, "Nationalism is a political system that places your country above every other in the scale of the world. Learn more about the system and how it compares from the rest of history and with other political systems." [1]

We are currently experiencing the impact of nationalism around the world. For instance, some have characterized the United States president, Mr. Trump, and his administration as a nationalist government, particularly when the president uses the phrase "America First." A similar view has been used to describe the nationalist trend in other parts of the world, including Europe, where it was attributed as a primary factor influencing Britain's decision to leave the European Union. The Guardian.com opinion page by Fintan O'Toole describes Britain's decision as "being driven by English nationalism" and further states, "it's not facetious: England seems to be stumbling towards a national independence it has scarcely even discussed, let alone prepared for. It is on the brink of one of history's strangest nationalist revolution."[2]

Shifting from Europe to the United States, divisions persist. In his book *American Nations*, Colin Woodard highlights the separate American historical and cultural factors that explain our divisions. He states that "After the revolution, four of the American nations hurdled the Appalachian and began spreading west across the Ohio and Mississippi valleys. There was very little mixing in their settlement streams, as politics, religion, ethnic prejudice, geography, and agricultural practices kept colonists

---

[1] Ann Sraders, (2018). What is nationalism? Its history and what it means in 2018, https://tinyurl.com/y9yk3rno

[2] O'Toole, Fintan. 2016. Brexit is being driven by English nationalism. And it will end in self-rule. *The Guardian.* https://www.theguardian.com/commentisfree/2016/jun/18/england-eu-referendum-brexit?CMP=share_btn_fb

almost entirely apart in four district tiers.".[3] Woodard further states, "Their respective cultural imprints can be seen to this date on maps created by linguists to trace American dialects, by anthropologists codifying material culture, and by political scientists tracing voting behaviors from the early nineteenth century straight through to the early twenty-first."

History repeats itself. Clearly, this replication of history and subsequent lack of people integrating and understanding one another as pointed out in Colin Woodard's book to some extent remains with us. I completely concur with Mr. Woodward that the historical divisions along with cultural factors cumulatively influence current divisions in our society, as demonstrated in our systemic discriminatory practices starting from our school system (urban and suburban), different communities (African American communities, Spanish communities, Asian-American communities, European-American communities, and of course, the economic classes (the have and the have-not communities). He particularly characterizes this circumstance as a time of "little mixing in their settlement streams, as politics, religion, ethnic prejudice, geography, and agricultural practices that kept colonists almost entirely apart in four district tiers."[4] To some extent, we witness the same in our local communities, which reflect a microcosm of our larger society, and are still noticeable in education, religion, politics, economics, jobs, lending systems, and especially in our criminal justice system.

Generally, these divisions can be viewed to some degree in almost all aspects of our society. For instance, in our education system, even after the landmark Supreme Court ruling *Brown v. Board of Education* outlawing segregation, some of our schools are still segregated today as they were prior to the ruling. It's clear that our schools and how we function in the context of existing inequity in school funding greatly reflects our relative preparation for success in life, how we live and operate in our communities and workplaces. We have not completely trusted one another, especially the older generations; therefore, discrimination remains ubiquitous in our society. Although there have been significant changes in terms of mingling

---

[3] Woodard, Colin. (2011). American Nations: A History of the Eleven Rival Regional Cultures of North America Kindle Edition. 173
[4] Ibid

and connecting between people from different cultures, we still have a long way to go to truly eradicate the divisions that are less overt, but certainly covertly drive the existing divisions and inequity in our society.

Clearly, as a society, we have not done enough. To even remotely begin to remedy these divisions, we need to be more open and honest about what separates us. Certainly, if we are not open in accepting the fact that we are not yet operating as one, as witnessed in our school funding that is largely allocated with bias towards certain zip codes, political connections, and other factors, it will be difficult for us to convince outsiders to believe us.

Divisions have largely led to the creation of a "we versus them" mentality (overtly or covertly), that has resulted in the lack of a meaningful dialogue. Otherwise, we would not have the kind of covert and overt discriminatory practices that inspire progressive organizations to continuously fight for equity and social justice for those who they believe the system discriminates against, as highlighted throughout this book. Careful analysis of racist and discriminatory practices in our system offers a clear explanation as to why advocates for equity and social justice for all feel that they cannot idly stand by while those who engage in discriminatory practices continue to do so. Especially when these discriminatory practices are directed towards African Americans and Hispanics Americans in our society, as shown by the Department of Justice report on Ferguson, Missouri, Baltimore, Maryland and elsewhere.[5]

Discriminatory practices are not new to the United States of America. Historically, we have witnessed and documented continued mistreatment of those who are perceived as not being "like us," which essentially contributes to and perpetuates unequal treatment, as in the case of three Department of Justice's investigative reports mentioned above. These forms of mistreatment come directly or indirectly, and each time we hear or read about courageous individuals or groups who fight against the system that perpetuates such pain, it gives us hope. For example, during the Civil

---

[5] Department of Justice report on the Ferguson, Mo. Police Department https://tinyurl.com/zfz9b97, Department of Justice report on Baltimore, Maryland https://tinyurl.com/zpgm3bk

Rights movement, courageous citizens, both black and white, confronted structural racism and discrimination that was rampant in our society. Some people gave their lives; these were true Americans, black and white together, fighting for equity and social justice for all.

When we fast forward from the turbulent 1960s, history is repeating itself. Organizations like Black Lives Matter are currently battling and courageously confronting a system that frequently and disproportionately mistreats African Americans and Hispanics. The Black Lives Matter Organization is courageously confronting and fighting for primary rights such as fair treatment for all, against those who have vehemently refused to abandon their racist beliefs. They are certainly an example of a progressive organization that sees the unfairness and mistreatment of some members of our society through overt or covert means. Courageous organizations such as Black Lives Matters couldn't idly stand any longer while they still witnessed the criminal justice system continuing unfair treatment to minorities. Advocacy for fair treatment and defending those they deem as being constantly discriminated against, particularly the minorities, is the primary purpose why organizations such as Black Lives Matter emerged in the first place. This overt discrimination is not limited to just law enforcement; there are also structural factors involved.

Taking an in-depth view on how both our larger and smaller contemporary communities live, a quick drive through in any neighborhood in the United States, whether rural, urban, or suburban, will offer you a clear indication that we are a people divided by either real or artificial walls. We are shaped and influenced by our experiences along the dimensions of race, class, ideation, politics, religion, urban and suburban, etc. These are some of the running issues discussed throughout this book.

Without going any further, I would particularly encourage you to pay close attention to the upcoming chapters, especially Chapters Two and Three, where I comprehensively discuss Belief Formation and Belief Transformation. The upcoming two chapters are foundational to the book. Chapter Two focuses on providing a framework for exploring and understanding the concept of belief formation, which is the basis for our belief system that influences all sorts of human behaviors. Chapter Two also deepens our understanding of our own belief system, based on our limited understanding of others that feeds and fosters the existing divisions in our society. On the other hand, Chapter Three illustrates the step-by-step process for transforming one's belief system.

Belief transformation provides the mechanism or process through which we address our misconceptions of one another and ultimately guides an individual through the development of a true and meaningful understanding of others. A process that is devoid of misconception provides a new and better enlightened belief system, which requires meaningful engagement with people, especially with those of whom we know very little or nothing about their life experiences. Therefore, knowing them and sharing experiences with them will enable us to strive towards sharing our common humanity and ultimately perfect this union we call the United States of America.

We live in different communities, and we engage in activities that don't always provide us the opportunities to truly get to know one another. Rather, we live in our confined communities with artificial walls that provide an environment that encourages the cultivation of the misconceptions we harbor about outsiders. This often leads to people making judgments about the people "residing" on the opposite side of the wall, and those they judge are often people they know little or nothing about. For example, not too long ago, we heard and read about executives at Texaco using racial epithets and making disparaging statements towards a segment of the minority population that the executives knew little or nothing about. The comments were based on the texture of African American hair and they made fun of a woman's hair. While the perpetrators, Texaco executives, enjoyed making fun of the woman's hair, the woman felt degraded and that by and large the experience impacted the African American woman negatively. In fact, she felt very uncomfortable.[6]

We do not even have to go far to see evidence of discriminatory practices in our society. In the example of Texaco's boardroom experience, these

---

[6] "Racism At Texaco". 1996. *Tinyurl.Com.* https://tinyurl.com/yca6eclk.

corporate executives engaged in comments that were disparaging and designed to be secret and fun among those that had developed a covert means to poke fun at what they knew to be inappropriate and unacceptable behavior. It happens that this is more covertly done today.

In this rare situation, the incident was caught on video. A *Christian Science Monitor* reporter provided evidence of what still happens in our private and public workplaces.[7] People from different groups engage in exclusive discussions that continuously shed light on our divisions that are driven by a "them versus us" mentality mindset. Practices such as Texaco's boardroom bigotry remain with us in one form or another. The public airing of tape recordings of Texaco top executives berating minority workers with racial epithets and planning to destroy documents related to a discrimination lawsuit brought against the oil giant is an example of discriminatory practice in corporate America. The *Christian Science Monitor* reflected on the incident based on the video recovered in a short statement:

> The tapes offer a rare, unfiltered look at senior executives of one major American corporation. However typical or atypical the comments may be, they highlight a problem of racism that many minorities believe remains deeply ingrained in the business world.[8]

Some would quickly dismiss the incident, citing that these transgressions occurred a long time ago and it was an isolated incident. Not so fast; there are numerous instances that suggest racism and xenophobia is well and alive in our society and it's one of the major contributing factors to the divisions viewed today. It is evident in our politics of the day. During the last presidential race, President Donald J. Trump called on the United States to bar all Muslims from entering the country until the

---

[7] Coolidge, Donald Shelley. 1996. Texaco Case Raises Red Flag For Companies Over Racism. CSmonitor.Com. https://www.csmonitor.com/1996/1108/110896.us.us.5.html
[8] Ibid

nation's leaders can "…figure out what is going on."[9] This was immediately after the terrorist attacks in San Bernardino, California, a position that is clearly an extraordinary escalation of rhetoric aimed at voters' fears about members of the Islamic faith. To understand this situation and the division it drives, one should understand Trump's proposal in a religious and Muslim extremist context, including different views that some believe but do not speak on publicly. For those who have suffered, and in some cases, subjected to undue discrimination, these incidents continue to plant the seeds of division.

As pointed out earlier, division in our society has always been historically documented. If something drastic is not done today, these issues will always be persistent. In her book, *The New Jim Crow*, Michelle Alexander pointed out a disturbing trend in our criminal justice or "injustice system" toward African Americans.[10] The book gives a stunning account of African Americans under the control of the criminal justice system, a situation Charles Blow cited in a *New York Times* article.[11]

According to Alexander, in certain cases, some individuals seem to discourage their relatives, especially children, from mixing or relating with others who are not like them. Sometimes we pretend by saying positive things in public places and yet behave differently in private situations. This is particularly confusing to children because they can see the inconsistencies in how some adults deliver public and private messages that are contradictory. Some people have the tendency to say harsh things about others in private and the opposite in public. For instance, imagine a situation in which a well-known professional engaging in a discussion characterized as a "parents dinner table discussion" – where parents tend to develop a two-dimensional approach to dealing with the issue of race:

---

[9] Johnson, Jenna. 2015. Trump calls for 'total and complete shutdown of Muslims entering the United States'. Washingtonpost.Com. https://www.washingtonpost.com/news/post-politics/wp/2015/12/07/donald-trump-calls-for-total-and-complete-shutdown-of-muslims-entering-the-united-states/

[10] Alexander, Michelle. "The New Jim Crow." Ohio St. J. Crim. L. 9 (2011): 7.

[11] Blow, Charles. 2012. "Opinion | Plantations, Prisons And Profits". *Tinyurl.Com.* http://tinyurl.com/hrkox4p.

1. the public and,
2. the private approach.

While in public, they use deceptive mechanisms to give the impression that they are friendly to people from different races or cultures, while in private, they discourage their children from relating or becoming friends with children that are different from them.

This situation persists and certainly is clear in our approach to changes in laws and in behaviors, making it a major problem today. Unfortunately, if we do not have courageous leaders who will honestly step up and tackle the issues associated with inequality and unfair treatment of minorities, we will not address these issues realistically. In fact, these issues remind me of Jack Nicholson's famous quote: "You want answers; you can't handle the truth!" from the movie *A Few Good Men*.[12]

Dealing with the truth means that it is time for America as a society to first accept the fact that racism and discrimination are abundant in our society, and that they comes in many forms. Consequently, we must then set goals that target discouraging racism and discrimination while tackling the problem of structural inequality and lack of social justice that is pervasive in our society. Careful evaluative analysis of what happens in our school systems reveals discriminatory school funding, different job opportunities involving people with similar qualifications, and what a student of mine illustrated this way: "It's no longer what you know that gets the bacon, it's who you know that does the trick." If we are serious about perfecting this union, we must attack the issues of inequity and nepotism in our society head on. If we do, we will catapult our society to where it should be. One great place to start is funding our schools and providing for all our children and not just some with quality teachers to reverse the foundational course of inequity in our system, especially in the formative years.

Clearly, if we intend to tackle and change the issues associated with bigotry and its derivatives, discrimination and inequality, we must start with education that is devoid of structural racism. Ranging from

---

[12] A Few Good Men. Reiner, Rob. Westwood. Columbia Pictures. 1992.

educational preparation of teachers and administrators to meaningfully tackling persistent equity gaps that continue to remind us of the previous discriminations such as the one reflected by Judge Debra M. Brown. In her ruling, Judge Brown ordered the Cleveland (Mississippi) School District to desegregate its schools after five decades of litigation.[13]

Recent reports on Senator Cindy Hyde-Smith in connection to segregation in Lawrence County Academy shed new light as to why the senator made the kind of comments she was criticized for making. The senator was recorded as saying, "If he invited me to a public hanging, I'd be on the front row."[14]

Furthermore, it was reported that,

> "Following the Supreme Court's 1969 mandate that America's public schools must immediately be desegregated — 15 years after the initial *Brown v. Board of Education* decision calling segregation unconstitutional — Lawrence County Academy in Monticello, Miss. was one of many high schools established in the South on behalf of white parents who did not want their children to be educated alongside black students. Lawrence County Academy opened one year after the Supreme Court's order, in 1970, the Free Press reported. Hyde-Smith graduated in 1977, meaning she would have been enrolled elsewhere at the time of the academy's founding, according to the Free Press."[15]

We must fight to prevent any further existence of a divided society as it is presently. In the next chapter, we will dive into belief formation, a crucial chapter that will provide the framework in our effort to understand

[13] Tess Owen (2016). Judge Orders Mississippi School District to Desegregate, Ending Decades-Long Fight (https://tinyurl.com/ydx6h54k)
[14] Forgery Quint, and James Arkin. 2018. "Mississippi Newspaper: Hyde-Smith Attended Segregation Academy". *POLITICO*. https://tinyurl.com/y8nb6ojx.
[15] Forgery Quint, and James Arkin. 2018. "Mississippi Newspaper: Hyde-Smith Attended Segregation Academy". *POLITICO*. https://tinyurl.com/y8nb6ojx.

why people behave the way they do and perhaps provide a step-by-step approach to understanding people. People's behaviors are shaped by certain circumstances they have no control over, and therefore, they should not be blamed or punished, but rather, we should understand and empathize with them, as well as help them navigate from a situation they have little or no control over to a situation of understanding and building bridges.

REFLECTION ON CHAPTER ONE

As you finish reading the chapter, please reflect on how it resonates with you in the context of your past, present, and how the future looks. Please consider the past and your present experience as you proceed. As you think through those experiences, be specific as to how the chapter relates to your unique experience. As you do, try to connect some of what you read to your own experience or the experience of other people that you know.

_____

_____

_____

_____

_____

_____

If you were able to relate or make connections, based on those connections you made, in what ways would you relay such powerful information to provide learning opportunities to others, especially young people?

_____

_____

_____

_____

_____

_____

In what ways has the content of this chapter helped you to ignite your metacognition while linking those experiences to multitudes of other experiences? As you reflect, please discuss how your experiences help foster meaningful understanding of the issues from one or more perspectives.

_____

_____

_____

_____

_____

_____

_____

If you have no relatable experience, please feel free to express that too. The aim of this chapter is to keep engaging with one another in exploring these issues. We cannot solve these issues by isolating them or pretending that they don't happen.

_____

_____

_____

_____

_____

_____

CHAPTER 2

BELIEF FORMATION PROCESS: WHAT INFORMS OUR BEHAVIORS?

What cultivates and nurtures our belief system? How does our belief system inform our conception of things? How does our conception of things propel us to do what we do? These are some of the questions we are going to explore in this chapter. Clearly, there are both good and bad behaviors and this chapter explores the factors that influence both. Finally, we will look further to gain a better understanding as to why people do what they do regardless of whether they share our perspective on certain issues or not. This will add value to our democratic process and foster meaningful debate on various issues. Our understanding of the factors that influence human behavior by extension propels us to become more understanding of the various forces influencing one's perspective, and thus helps us to become more tolerant and sympathetic to behaviors that may not be consistent with our own belief system.

Our belief system is the core driver of our behavior. This remains the case regardless of whether it is good or bad behavior. Our belief system is largely the function of our environment, culture, values, and institutions such as schools and churches; it simply reflects our conception of things from childhood to adulthood. The diagram below shows the conceptual framework of one's belief system informed by human experiences. Read the diagram in a clockwise direction. Each step shows how we connect and interact with our environment and culture, which in turn cumulatively influences the formation our beliefs ingrain in our schemata. Our schemata is a conceptual framework that organizes and serves as the infrastructure of experiences guiding human behavior. It also provides for adaptation of human behavior from simple to complex circumstances as highlighted throughout this book.

Belief Formation Process:

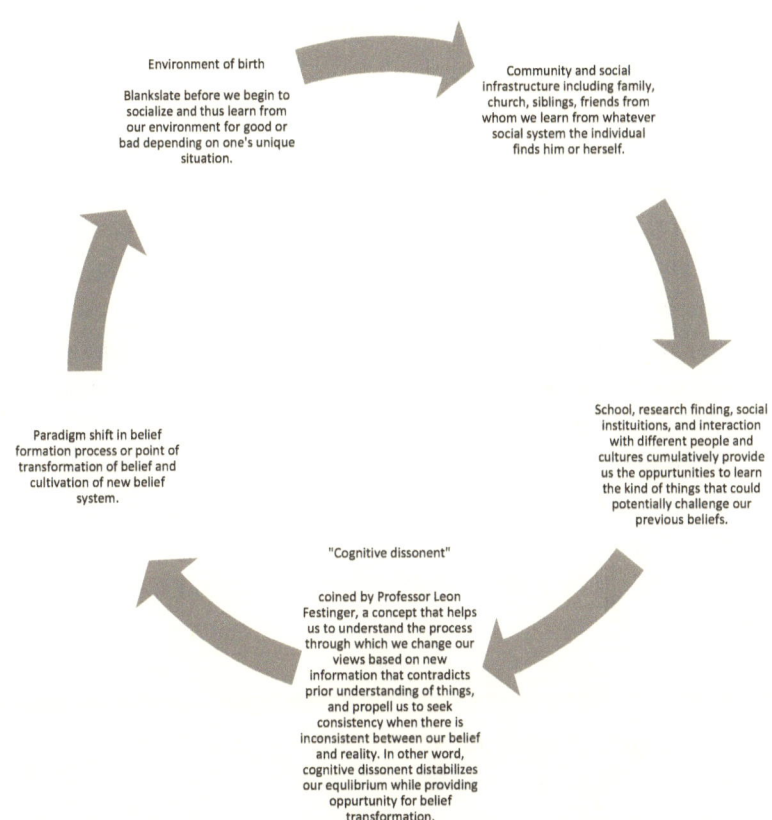

Environment of birth

Blankslate before we begin to socialize and thus learn from our environment for good or bad depending on one's unique situation.

Community and social infrastructure including family, church, siblings, friends from whom we learn from whatever social system the individual finds him or herself.

School, research finding, social institutions, and interaction with different people and cultures cumulatively provide us the oppurtunities to learn the kind of things that could potentially challenge our previous beliefs.

Paradigm shift in belief formation process or point of transformation of belief and cultivation of new belief system.

"Cognitive dissonent"

coined by Professor Leon Festinger, a concept that helps us to understand the process through which we change our views based on new information that contradicts prior understanding of things, and propell us to seek consistency when there is inconsistent between our belief and reality. In other word, cognitive dissonent distabilizes our equilibrium while providing oppurtunity for belief transformation.

One's belief system is a function of the individual's collective internal and external experiences, which includes and isn't limited to family, culture, race, norm, religion, gender, and ideation. For example, when someone is born in a rural, urban, or suburban area, they are normally surrounded by people and experiences within that particular environment. The people, experiences, and community in general cumulatively shape the individual's belief system because they share the same values. In such situations, the individual's belief system will be formed by the cultural values and institutions, such as schools and churches.

To illustrate, let's use the same recent drama involving Senator Cindy Hyde-Smith where she spoke about her willingness to attend public hangings if invited to one. In the statement, the senator was reflecting on the culture of her state, Mississippi.[16] The state has been particularly characterized as the worst when it comes to the inhuman way African Americans were treated during Jim Crow days. Michelle Alexander eloquently describes this events in her book, *The New Jim Crow*.[17]

You would think that no one would make inflammatory and inciting statements or remarks, especially because these remarks are a painful reminder to the victims of lynching and their loved ones of outrageously inhuman acts perpetuated against African American victims, and by extension, their relatives. Only the perpetrators, their sympathizers, and those who never understood the anguish victims went through could make insensitive and derogatory comments associated with the dark days for African Americans. For the senator, such comments would be normal and a reflection of how she was brought up. She probably had always been around people who made similar comments and laughed them off without considering how harmful and hurtful these comments can be perceived as it appears to be the case when a journalist pursued and asked the senator to explain.

Of course, the senator could not explain because she has not realized what public hanging meant to victims or the pain and anguish and how relatives of the victims still feel about what their dear ones went through. If she understood such pain, she wouldn't have made them, even if she felt that way. Her statement was a shocker, especially for those who know and understand the term "lynching" in the context of this nation's racist dark

---

[16] Quint Forgey (2018). Mississippi newspaper: Hyde-Smith attended segregation academy Politico.com https://tinyurl.com/y8nb6ojx

[17] Alexander, Michelle. "The New Jim Crow." Ohio St. J. Crim. L. 9 (2011): 7.

history. Although she apologized for those who were hurt by the statement, she still comes from a state known for racist behavior. She attended a school that was designed to circumvent the law banning segregation and admitted only white students.

Numerous reports seemed to confirm that the senator had also sent her own daughter to a similar school. She made it seem she went ahead and played an active role in sustaining segregated schools in Mississippi. Her racially charged statements and choice of school for her daughter clearly show that the senator was acting on what she knew and felt based on her experience. As a result, she used the statement to garner support from those people that share similar racist culture and values that shaped her belief system. These are the very people that also share the belief that segregation of children, particularly preventing black and white children from going to the same school or mixing was okay. To understand the impact of the senator's experience, which was pivotal in shaping her belief system, one should put it all in context of time and cultural value. Keep in mind that this is a woman who lived in the era when her state government and the people within the community were engaging in activities that could be considered as racist and illegal. The Mississippi governor characterized the state as having "a history of supporting racial segregation," as well as habitual instances of circumventing and refusing to comply with a federal court order to finally desegregate its public schools.

Throughout the senator's upbringing, she lived, learned, and associated with racists, people who designed their own schools to keep white schools separate with the purpose of countering the 1954 *Brown v Board of Education* ruling that outlawed segregation. The senator should not be blamed completely for her state's position on the issue of race, neither should she be blamed for her parents' decision to send her to such a school, even though it was the kind of school she chose to send her child, something that was revealed by the *Daily Journal* reporter, Caleb Bedillion. The reporter felt that the senator should, however, be held accountable not only for sending her child to a segregated school, but also for her recent comments that are characterized by many as being racist.[18]

Let's explore other examples as to how people form their belief system. We previously alluded to the view that in order to understand one's belief system, one must become familiar with the cultural values, biases, and institutions that cumulatively shape one's belief. Every individual or group is shaped by his or her own experiences. Everyone within any culture has culturally specific knowledge of his or her group, and those variables combine to shape the person's belief system. One's belief system is a function of the individual's cultural experiences, as exemplified by "Derek Black's" life experience.

In a piece by Ali Saslow of the *Washington Post* (Oct. 16, 2016), he described the life of Derek Black, a young white man who was influenced by his racist parents and the culture of hate in which he was schooled.[19] Derek was referenced by Ali as an impressive, intelligent, and articulate young man who was indoctrinated into a racist belief system. According to Ali, Derek's parents clearly provided him with the tools to hate blacks and Jews, especially during his developmental years, which Ali described as a less-than-idyllic culture. Derek grew up within a culture that ultimately influenced his belief system. A belief system sheds light and explains what led to Derek's hate towards certain people. He learned to hate. No one is born to hate.

In Ali Saslow's piece, he profiled Mr. Don Black, who had grown up in Alabama and joined a group called the "White Youth Alliance" in the 1970s. This group was led by David Duke, who at the time was married or associated with Chloe (Derek's mother). Based on the article, Chloe was married to David Duke, the former head of the Ku Klux Klan. Clearly, David Duke's relationship with Don and Chloe and common association subsequently led to a new relationship between Don Black and Chloe, a

---

[18] Caleb Bedillion (2018) CALEB BEDILLION: National Spotlight Prompts Personal Probing. Daily Journal https://tinyurl.com/yanhnm2x
[19] Ali Saslow (Oct. 16, 2016), The White Flight of former New College student Derek Black. Washington Post https://tinyurl.com/y8lk92u7

union that gave birth to Derek Black in 1989, who of course was trained to hate by his racist parents, according to Ali.[20]

Ali further narrated Derek's experience, which led him to learn about hate. As Derek got to school, Don Black and Chloe (his parents) did not want their kid being taught by a black teacher, so they pulled Derek out of school to go to an elementary school close to his mother's home. The family moved into Chloe's childhood home in West Palm, along with Chloe's two young daughters. Don and Derek always associated and socialized with Don's friends from the white power movement, something that soon began influencing Derek. In the article, Ali described Derek's father as having referenced his son as possessing "all my strengths without any of my weaknesses." Digging deeper, you will find out the connection that existed between Derek Black's father and mother and their relationship with KKK leader David Duke. Here is your answer – they connect and the impact of the company one keeps, intentionally or unintentionally, shapes one's behavior (like father, like son.)

According to *Washington Post* writer Ali Saslow, "He was not only a leader of racial politics but also a product of it." Derek's father, Don Black, had created Stormfront, the internet's first and largest white nationalist site with 300,000 users and counting. According to the *Washington Post* writer, Derek's mother was associated with one of the country's most infamous racial zealots, David Duke.[21] Based on Derek's friends, family, and environment as well as his social cultural development, what he became could be characterized as predictable. He was surrounded by racists, who greatly influenced him and his views. They raised Derek at the forefront of the movement and some white nationalists had begun to call him "the heir." The story of Derek is the story of how humans form their belief systems that by and large drive behaviors whether good or bad.

Although we have seen how cultural upbringing shaped Don, Chloe, and subsequently their child, Derek, other phenomena could also impact

---

[20] Ali Saslow (Oct. 16, 2016), The White Flight of former New College student Derek Black. Washington Post https://tinyurl.com/y8lk92u7
[21] Ibid

human behavior. This situation describes how experience influences human behavior in a similar way in which it underscores the power of the belief formation diagram in shaping behaviors. For instance, an article in the *New York Times* by Campbell Robertson followed up on the discussion he had heard.

> "Pastors, theologians and sociologists were talking of how black worshipers were leaving white-majority churches. They were leaving quietly, a family here, a single person there. But it was happening everywhere, a movement large enough for some to see the unraveling of decades of efforts at racial reconciliation."[22]

Campbell set about inquiring as to the reasons why black worshipers were leaving white-majority churches. The search was quite easy, as he was able to gather important and relevant information on Facebook from blacks that had left the predominately white churches and the reasons why they had left. In his own words, Campbell explained the reasons as being:

> "I would find someone on Facebook, a black worshiper who had posted about leaving a predominately white church and another going through the same situation halfway across the country. They would both think they were going through this alone, yet their accounts on the matter would be remarkably similar."

Campbell continued explaining:

> "People spoke to me of being tired, let down, heartbroken. Political and cultural partitions that they had long overlooked at worship time now overshadowed every service."

---

[22] Campbell Robertson. 2018. At the Crossroads of Church and Race, a Reporter Glimpses His Childhood. New York Times. https://www.nytimes.com/2018/03/09/us/church-race-segregation.html

Campbell further figured that the realizations almost always began after the death of Trayvon Martin in 2012, and a sense that white church leaders or fellow worshipers did not want to talk about how a black teenager walking home from a 7-Eleven could end up dead. Sometimes the preacher would privately express sympathy, but also showed some reservation and concern how his white congregation would take the remarks. Campbell further stated:

> "Then the Trump election came, with its troubling racial overtones. For many, it wasn't even complicated at that point. They just stopped going."

In both instances above, it's clear that both blacks and white are driven to act based on their experiences buttressed by the unanswered question: "How could a black teenager walking home from a 7-Eleven end up dead?" On one hand, a pastor and some members of the congregation would discuss privately and sympathize about what happens to blacks, but on the other hand, the same people shunned discussing the same topic in public. These are all part of the problems stemming from divisions that impede true conversation and perhaps solutions to real issues that we are all faced with.

It is fitting to bring Mark Twain's assertion that one is the company one keeps, and by extension, it is evident in Derek's belief formation process: "Where you live really does shape who you are." We can now conclude that the community in which Senator Cindy Hyde-Smith grew up shaped her and that's who she is and that's how her belief system was cultivated. This is a theme that runs throughout the history of racism in our nation, and is explored further in subsequent chapters.

In Chapter Three, we will be exploring belief transformation and its power as a road map to shaping a better and inclusive society. The diagram below will further show the impact of one's experience in shaping his or her behavior.

The Formation of Belief Systems

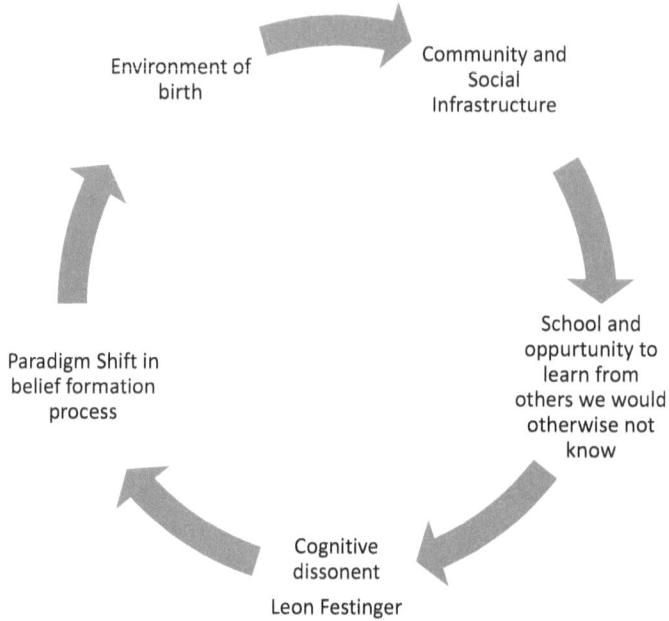

The days of misconception and mistreatment of others are long gone. We must learn to see each other and act by "The Golden Rule Principle" (treat others the way you would like people to treat you) towards one another in our global communities.

Globalization has substantially increased opportunities for people to engage with others outside their constrained environment, perfectly fitting into Mark Twain's view that "Where you live really does shape who you are." Today, people are moving around, observing, and interacting with other people from all over the world, in some cases instantaneously through technology and ubiquitous multimedia platforms. The internet has cumulatively opened opportunities to exchange ideas and learn from each other.

Our experiences are no longer limited to where we live. They are garnered from the unlimited global community resources that we have access to. With a new environment and new exposure from continued interaction with different environments and cultures, our personality cumulatively influences our belief systems, which in turn influence how one behaves. I believe that every individual's experience could be somewhat be attributed to what shaped the person they turned out to be. Reflecting on my own personal experience, I can also get a view of how those experiences informed my behavior just like everyone else.

During my formative years at Nawfia, a small town in Anambra State of Nigeria, I interacted with so many people from different countries and cultures. I came from a family of eight siblings, four boys and four girls. Our parents focused on instilling in all of us the value of education and respect for others, especially those who were older. These values undoubtedly shaped and continue to influence my behavior in all that I do. I learned so much from those experiences.

Things were certainly different from here, where children have buses literally picking them up from their homes. During my days in Nigeria, we would walk to school with friends every day, interacting and sharing stories. We knew what everyone else was doing, who they were, their parents, siblings, and where they lived. It was a very connected community and neighbors looked out for one another. Pretty much everyone knew how he or she was expected to act. You never did anything in the presence of your neighbors that you wouldn't want your parents or teachers to know about because they would be informed by whoever saw you. Parents within the community collectively parented all the children. They discussed each child's behaviors, praised and corrected when necessary. In other words, good deeds were praised not just by one's parents, but by all adults within the community, and of course, if one behaved badly, the person got punished accordingly by the adult members of the community.

Perhaps this might be the reason why the former United States Secretary of State and Democratic Presidential Candidate for the 2016 presidential elections, Hillary Clinton, used the expression "It takes a village." Clearly those walks and exchanges of ideas, the school, family, and the entire community engagement with everyone influenced who I am today and certainly could explain my perspective on life.

Those experiences in that small town are not unique to me and the people I grew up with; it applies to everyone in any community. Perhaps the different cultural experiences influence the differences we see amongst people from different places on earth. In other words, it applies to everyone, based on individual or group circumstances and cultural differences. Each individual or group of people is the embodiment of all their experiences that ultimately form their belief system. For one to truly understand other people, it's important to imagine being in their shoes, which means experiencing what they have experienced and genuinely asking how you would feel or act if you were them. This could give you a sense of why people are different and behave differently.

As I indicated earlier, the process of belief formation is not unique to any individual or a group of an individual's culture; it applies to everyone based on special circumstances and cultural differences. Each society or individual within it gains cultural specific knowledge, which provides the window through which we can understand why people behave the way they do. Now that we have come to the end of this chapter, I encourage readers to keep in mind the belief formation process and the role the diagram plays in providing the framework for each person's behavior.

The next chapter will focus on Belief Transformation, which focuses on the process of changing or modifying one's belief system, which is sometimes subtle and sometimes turns out to be quite dramatic. Before we move to the chapter on Belief Formation, let's reflect on this chapter to assess what we have gained and how it could help us moving forward in life's journey.

REFLECTION ON THE CHAPTER

As you finish reading the chapter, please reflect on how it resonates with you in the context of your past, present, and how the future looks. Please consider the past and your present experience as you proceed. As you think through those experiences, be specific as to how the chapter relates to your unique experience, and as you do, try to connect some of what you read to your own experience or the experience of other people that you know.

_____

_____

_____

_____

_____

_____

_____

If you were able to relate or make connections, based on those connections you made, in what ways would you relay such powerful information to provide learning opportunities to others, especially the young people?

_____

_____

_____

_____

_____

_____

_____

In what ways has the content of this chapter helped you to ignite your metacognition while linking those experiences to multitudes of other experiences? As you reflect, please discuss how your experiences help foster meaningful understanding of the issues from one or more perspectives.

_____

_____

_____

_____

_____

_____

_____

If you have no relatable experience, please feel free to express that too. The aim of this chapter is to keep engaging with one another in exploring these issues. We cannot solve these issues by isolating them or pretending that they don't happen.

_____

_____

_____

_____

_____

_____

_____

CHAPTER 3

BELIEF TRANSFORMATION: HOW INTERACTIVE AND EXPLORATIVE ENGAGEMENT WITH PEOPLE WHO ARE DIFFERENT FROM US ENHANCE OUR EXPERIENCE, KNOWLEDGE AND THE QUALITY OF OUR DECISIONS.

In the second chapter, we focused on the belief formation process and concluded that one's beliefs are a function of the individual's behavior. Belief transformation is a function of new information or experiences that engineer a paradigm shift in one's perspective. Basically, we are the company we keep, and the more we expand it with people whose cultural perspectives are different from ours, the more likely that those new and differentiated experiences will propel one to a paradigm shift, transforming one's belief in general.

It's the composition of the company one keeps that plays a significant role in one's belief transformation process and ultimately one's behavior. In other words, one's beliefs inform his or her behavior, and rarely can anyone separate their beliefs from their behavior. We are all shaped in one way or another by our experiences. One's belief system is a function of the individual's collective internal and external experiences that include, among others, family, culture, race, religion, gender, and ideation. Further, exposure to new ideas and especially those attached to compelling experiences that may stem from open engagement, exploration of ideas, and exchanging information drives transformation of one's belief system. Mark Twain's view applied then and is still relevant in today's global world where technological advancement and multimedia has expanded and extended the potential for cultural difference to influence the transformation of belief processes.

Like belief formation, belief transformation is driven by new experiences or knowledge that provide the rationale for one to modify his or her belief or outright change. This mainly is because the previous experiences or knowledge aren't enough to tackle current issues. The good news, though, is that we now have the ability and means to engage with people of various backgrounds and geographical locations. Interaction with various experiences and company prepare people to function more effectively in our global community and provides an opportunity for them to transform earlier belief. Belief formation and belief transformation are in many ways similar in the sense that they are both shaped by experience. The difference, though, is that belief transformation occurs as a result of someone changing their mind based on new information that compels them to abandon old beliefs stemming from misconception, therefore embracing new beliefs through the belief transformation process.

In a belief transformation, one encounters real challenges that compel them to change their earlier belief and embrace a new one or modifies the old (belief transformation). This situation is usually triggered by a traumatic experience or revelation that challenges what one had believed to be true, only to realize through new information that it is not so or, at a minimum, questionable.

To further understand the power of belief transformation, we have to analyze belief transformation by focusing on belief formation based on the misconception one developed from childhood and subsequently corrected the misconception through infusion of new information that ultimately changes their belief system. As we gather new and more authentic information, we are pushed towards questioning our earlier conception of things that are not in sync with our belief system, causing us to embrace a new perspective. We are propelled to modify, change, or transform our beliefs.

Shared history, ideas, values, norms, and culture, along with the values shared by family and peers, are paramount in the formation of our belief system. These are the people closest to us. We normally trust them, and they are often the source of our inspiration. These accumulated experiences we gain from those we love, trust, and respect ultimately shape our belief system, and by extension, influence our behavior. We tend to follow their footsteps by doing exactly what they expect from us based on the shared values and cultures.

In recent research, a reporter, Graeme Paton, Education Correspondent of the *British Telegraph*, asserts that the greatest influence on human behavior, especially for children, comes not from their parents, but from their peers. This is particularly true, as shown throughout the report. The report shows that children, especially in their formative years, can easily be convinced by others to do things their parents would disapprove of. Children are drawn to one another; they play together and share common interests within the company they keep, therefore supporting Graeme Paton's assertion that children are influenced by their peers more than their parents.[23]

The power of peer influence on one's behavior is significant. Take for instance in the United States where Christian children are introduced to Santa Claus in a social environment and hence develop a belief system that Santa is real. Clearly, the child's introduction to Santa shaped by the child's experience with Santa along with other children and the company one keeps helps in shaping one's belief system in the context of how he or she perceives the meaning of Santa Claus. If you were born and nurtured in the United States, you probably grew up believing in Santa Claus with

[23] Graeme, Paton. 2007. Children 'Learn Most From Peers Not Parents'. Telegraph. Co.Uk. https://tinyurl.com/ycpbpnr6

other children. You were perhaps convinced along with others to believe in the power of Santa Claus and his ability to shower you with great presents. The influence of peers and loved ones in shaping behavior is evident during Christmas time. Loved ones have led children to embrace misconceptions. Children have the propensity to accept this misconception as if it's true because they are prone to believing in the people they love and trust at that time. Such misconceptions, as in case of Santa, stay with the person as they grow up. When children learn there is no Santa Claus, they feel betrayed by the person they were led to love, trust, and believe in. They believed in what they were taught to believe (illustration of belief formation process).

Belief Transformation

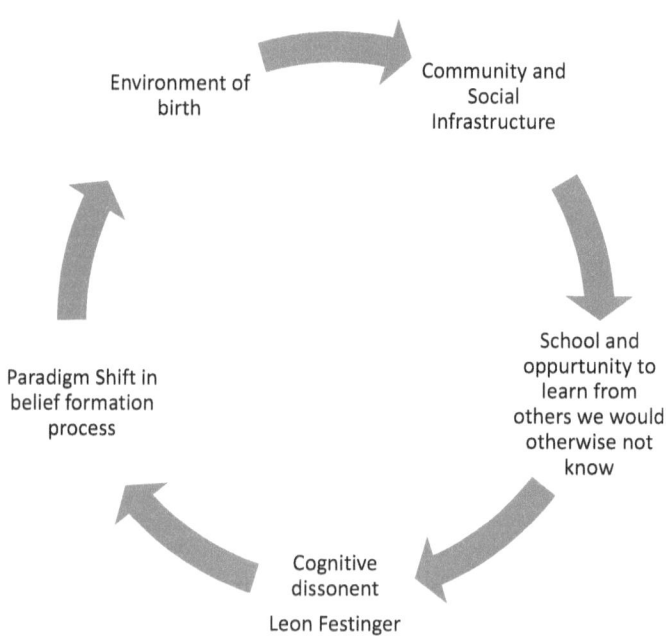

Belief transformation means a change of one's belief to something new based on new information. Let us amplify the process of belief formation and subsequently demonstrate how new experience propels one to change or transform his or her belief. This scenario will serve as a scaffolder and a follow-up to the earlier discussion on belief formation based on the misconception of Santa Claus. In this situation, explore the concept of belief formation, and subsequently, belief transformation from the point of view of a child to an adult. Assume that you have realized that the stories that you were told about Santa Claus were based on misconception, which is another way of accepting what is not true as if it is. However, you start to realize the whole misconception and what you had always believed as result of what you were taught as a child. As you grew up, you probably wondered as why and what you knew of Santa Claus is now being challenged, and that could therefore lead a child to begin questioning the whole idea of Santa Claus and why they were lied to about Santa Claus being real.

This situation shows the beginnings of cognitive dissonance, when you find out that what you were told about Santa Claus was neither true nor real. As a result, you begin to transform your previous belief system from the old to new beliefs through research. With this new understanding about Santa Claus, you change your view to reflect current research, reality, or new findings as new truth is revealed in the transformation process (see transformational diagram).

The quest to use new information in our new belief system aligns with John Dewey's view when he stated, "As new discoveries are made, new truths disclosed, and new opinions change with change of circumstances, instructions must change also and keep pace with time".[24] Clearly, the concept of acquiring new and authentic information leads to a change in terms of new perspective that uncovers the facts and authentic information that propels one to embrace the concept of belief transformation. It provides opportunity for addressing other misconceptions, especially those associated with social issues.

The transformation of belief becomes an essential concept that enables us to foster the change we need to in order to reflect what's real and the true nature of things. This book also addresses misconceptions in other areas, such as gender, race, etc. to enable us to reverse those unacceptable behaviors that should be subject to belief transformation, including racism, gender inequality, religious discrimination, and all other forms of discriminatory practices that are present in our society.

---

[24] John Dewey. (1939). Freedom and Culture, 1939, p. 157).

Diagram on Belief Transformation Process

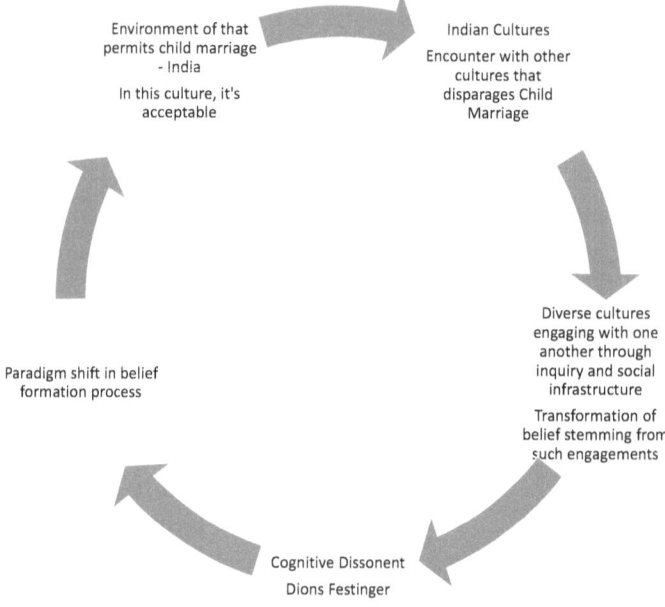

Environment of that permits child marriage - India

In this culture, it's acceptable

Indian Cultures

Encounter with other cultures that disparages Child Marriage

Diverse cultures engaging with one another through inquiry and social infrastructure

Transformation of belief stemming from such engagements

Paradigm shift in belief formation process

Cognitive Dissonent

Dions Festinger

As pointed out in the previous chapter, we are shaped by our experiences, which in turn inform our behavior. For instance, if you are a young black male in an urban environment, you may constantly see how fellow blacks are mistreated when compared with their counterparts who are white. Imagine being a young black man, reading newspapers, research from reputable institutions along with evening news headlining stories involving young black men being stopped by police often without any reason, observing different treatment of blacks in classrooms, disproportionate discipline, and suspension of black children compared to other racial groups. These news pieces have been documented by Claudia Rowe of the *Seattle Times* and Donna St. George of the *Washington Post*, and NPR, among others. The truth is that after some time, your belief system will reflect your observations and you will slowly begin to believe it, and subsequently, it will influence your entire belief system and how you behave.

Similarly, if you are a Muslim and consistently experience Muslim Americans being referred to as terrorists and every so often come across discriminatory actions motivated simply because one is a Muslim, at some point, these experiences will begin to impact upon your belief system, and subsequently, your behavior. For instance, prior to the recent presidential election in 2016, Republican nominee and current president, Donald J. Trump, called for the United States to bar all Muslims from entering the country until the nations' leaders can "figure out what is going on."[25]

President Trump's comment about Muslims during the elections was not made in complete isolation. These comments were a made as a direct response to the terrorist attacks in San Bernardino, California. The problem, though, was that barring all Muslims from entering the country was generalizing and castigating an entire group based on the actions of very few individuals. Such behavior never solves any problem but instead amplifies the situation toward the members of the Islamic faith, which thus fosters even bigger division on religious grounds. These comments seem to have instigated local attack on Muslims and their properties.

Singling out a religious group clearly violates equal protection under the law and it would be interpreted as such, especially for those who have experienced mistreatment. It certainly negates a famous quote by the founders of this nation when they stated, "We hold these truths to be self-evident, that all men are created equal, that they are endowed by their Creator with certain unalienable rights, that among these are life, liberty, and the pursuit of happiness."[26] Furthermore, such mistreatment of people based on religion or race is a clear violation of the victim's 14th Amendment of the United States Constitution, which grants equal protection under the law to all citizens regardless of race, gender, religion, etc.

As we come to the end of this chapter, I encourage you to continuously think how this chapter relates to the previous chapter on belief formation. Through reflection on both chapters and engagement in the relationship between these two concepts, you can link the same to metacognition

---

[25] Johnson, Jenna. 2015. Trump calls for 'total and complete shutdown of Muslims entering the United States'. Washingtonpost.Com. https://www.washingtonpost.com/news/post-politics/wp/2015/12/07/donald-trump-calls-for-total-and-complete-shutdown-of-muslims-entering-the-united-states/
[26] U.S. Declaration of Independence, 1776.

activities in exploration and inquiry and see why those two chapters are crucial in learning and understanding human behavior. As a result, you will gain deeper understanding as to why we should all embrace the Golden Rule principles and treat others how we would want to be treated. However, before we go to the next chapter, let's reflect on what we have learned from this chapter.

REFLECTION ON THE CHAPTER

As you finish reading the chapter, please reflect on how it resonates with you in context of your past, present, and how the future looks. Please consider the past and your present experience as you proceed. As you think through those experiences, be specific as to how the chapter relates to your unique experience. Try to connect some of what you read to your own experience or the experience of other people that you know.

_____

_____

_____

_____

_____

_____

_____

If you were able to relate or make connections, based on those connections you made, in what ways would you relay such powerful information to provide learning opportunities to others, especially young people?

_____

_____

_____

_____

_____

_____

_____

In what ways has the content of this chapter helped you to ignite your metacognition while linking those experiences to multitudes of other experiences? As you reflect, please discuss how your experiences help foster meaningful understanding of the issues from one or more perspectives.

If you have no relatable experience, please feel free to express that too. The aim of this chapter is to keep engaging with one another in exploring these issues. We cannot solve these issues by isolating them or pretending that they don't happen.

CHAPTER 4

GENDER BELIEF FORMATION AND THE NEED FOR BELIEF TRANSFORMATION

In spite of generalized efforts to eradicate gender bias and the subsequent inequity in our society, it still remains with us. Often we observe, read, or see things that suggest gender-motivated bias, which is like a never-ending story. Gender inequality refers to unequal treatment or a negative perception of women based entirely upon gender. It is a social construct usually arising from gender-biased roles that society assigns to people. The unfair roles the society places on people is a function of society's misconception that men outperform women in almost all aspects of life.

A recent case of gender bias at Google propelled national and international media to address the issue of gender inequity present in our society and globally. Gender inequality is an ongoing discussion taking place almost everywhere, including local libraries, bookstores, newspapers articles, magazines/journals features, and of course television shows. Two incidents however, stand out, one of them being the Elain Powell's lawsuit against Google. Ms. Powell sued Google for discriminatory practices that she felt manifested themselves in different forms, including being excluded from meetings, as well as other important events. She asserts that the discriminatory practices reached to a point where they were obvious and pervasive, something that led her to file a sixteen-million-dollar lawsuit against Google. She didn't win, despite the pain she endured from the real or perceived exclusion in regular work-related activities.[27]

The mere fact that the litany of the atrocious mistreatment of women and the conception that it is happening, and it is predicted to continue to happen, encouraged and drove Ms. Powell to continue to fight as much as she could for such behavior to be exposed and addressed. In Ms. Powell's recent interview by NPR correspondent by Terry Gross, she provided information on what she endured, including humiliation and subjugation to a second-class citizen just because she happened to be a woman. In one episode, she asserts that her entire team comprised of white men, most of their discussion centered on porn stars and untasteful banter on sex acts. At the time, she expressed how she wondered how long it would take her to get out of that situation where white men consistently made disparaging statements about women. Powell felt that the perpetrators lacked sensitivity and certainly didn't realize how what they were doing impacted others, especially women.

Gender discrimination and subjugation is pervasive in our society. Even technology companies are now acknowledging that it exists. In fact, Google has been accused of other extreme gender inequities, specifically differential pay, as shown in the United States Department of Labor reports. Google's defense against gender inequality allegations was a statement that addressed the company's difficulty or rather inability to provide data on gender inequality.[28] This is because this information would provide irrefutable evidence of gender inequity in pay, that women are paid up to 13% less than men. The unfair pay differential data clearly showed the extent of inequity towards women.[29]

---

[27] Levin, Sam. 2017. Google accused of 'extreme' gender pay discrimination by US labor department. *The Guardian.* https://www.theguardian.com/technology/2017/apr/07/google-pay-disparities-women-labor-department-lawsuit

[28] Levin, Sam. 2017. Google accused of 'extreme' gender pay discrimination by US labor department. *The Guardian.* https://www.theguardian.com/technology/2017/apr/07/google-pay-disparities-women-labor-department-lawsuit

[29] Levin, Sam. 2017. Google accused of 'extreme' gender pay discrimination by US labor department. *The Guardian.* https://www.theguardian.com/technology/2017/apr/07/google-pay-disparities-women-labor-department-lawsuit

In a different case at Google, an employee made disparaging statements against women, suggesting that men by and large outperform women, performance that he attributed to gender differences.[30] These recent instances at Google provide informational data, including a situation in which Google's engineers pushed the false narrative that men are naturally programmed to outperform women, is not unique. These statements are a continuation of propaganda designed to subjugate women to second-class citizens.

Clearly, the subjugating of women in our society is not a new phenomenon. Former Harvard University president Larry Summers once suggested that men's performance over women can be attributed to gender differences. In his speech at a conference hosted by the National Bureau of Economic Research, Mr. Summers explained that the reason for shortage of women in senior posts in science and engineering could be attributed to gender differences. He further associated the lack of women in science and engineering to women's responsibilities in childcare among other reasons.[31]

Summer's disapproving and indefensible comments led to at least half of the conference attendees, who were women, to walk out because they found these remarks very offensive. In response to Summer's remark, Denise Denton, who later became the President of the University of California at Santa Cruz, responded by saying, "It was really shocking to hear the president of Harvard make statements like that." Another conference attendee stated, "Mr. Summer's comments were depressingly familiar." Another woman pointed out that she had heard men make such comments her entire life. She said, "Quite honestly, if I had listened, I would never have done anything."[32]

The issue of gender inequity and persistent differential treatment of women was further seen in the 2016 presidential election, when Hillary Clinton's

---

[30] Chuck, Elizabeth. 2018. "Google Engineer Fired For Writing Manifesto On Women's 'Neuroticism' Sues Company". *NBC News.* https://tinyurl.com/ycd37qs2.
[31] Goldenberg, Suzanne. 2005. Why women are poor at science, by Harvard president. *The Guardian.* https://www.theguardian.com/science/2005/jan/18/educationsgendergap.genderissues
[32] Goldenberg, Suzanne. 2005. Why women are poor at science, by Harvard president. *The Guardian.* https://www.theguardian.com/science/2005/jan/18/educationsgendergap.genderissues

campaign was strongly denigrated and she was labeled as someone who could not be trusted because of the private e-mail scandal. President Trump's camp spoke vehemently against Hillary Clinton's use of her private e-mail, and now that they are in power, they are doing the same thing they accused Hillary Clinton of doing. Some have argued that the way Hillary Clinton was mistreated for her e-mails and a host of other things reflected differential treatment of women in the workplace. Unfortunately, gender inequity does not only occur in one field. It also extends to the legal profession, as seen in the case filed by Andrus Anderson on behalf of a former attorney in a nationwide class action against Steptoe & Johnson. The lawsuit alleges that the firm pays only "lip service" to diversity in its workforce, and subjects its "female attorneys to unequal pay." In the suit, Plaintiff Ji-In Houck alleges that her $85,000 starting salary was half that of male lawyers fresh out of law school, who were paid $165, 000."[33]

This chapter tries to find out and understand what propels people to cultivate their belief formation and how these beliefs influence the development of gender bias and subsequently discrimination toward women in academia, jobs, promotions, and yes, pay differentials.

In Chapters Two and Three, we focused on the belief system and how it influences our behavior. A similar argument suffices here, where discriminatory practices against women in all aspects of their lives can be attributed to societally constructed biased ideas that somehow one's gender drives what role that society assigns to the person. Besides understanding the belief formation process that drives human behavior, we also explore the belief transformation process that ultimately helps to transform the old, biased belief system of fear to positive views of women, to transition to a new belief system fostering equity and social justice for all, regardless of their gender. Considering these obvious inequities supported by research and evidenced by instances of differential pay, it suffices that we pose an important question to further explore what cultivates and nurtures those false premises that women are lesser beings.

---

[33] Debenedictis, Don. 2017. Class Action Accuses Steptoe & Johnson of Gender Bias. *Court House News*. https://www.courthousenews.com/class-action-accuses-steptoe-johnson-gender-bias/

To that end, let us begin by exploring the formation of a gender belief system. As it has been clear from the beginning of this book, especially in Chapters Two and Three, one's belief system is the core driver of the individual's behavior; and that remains the case regardless of whether it is about race, gender, socio-economic, religion, etc. The same is true when it comes to the issue of gender and why women are subjugated to second-class citizens; these are pertinent and important issues in the context of gender inequity. Before we go any further, let us spend some time exploring and understanding the process of belief formation as illustrated in the diagram below:

Belief Formation Diagram.

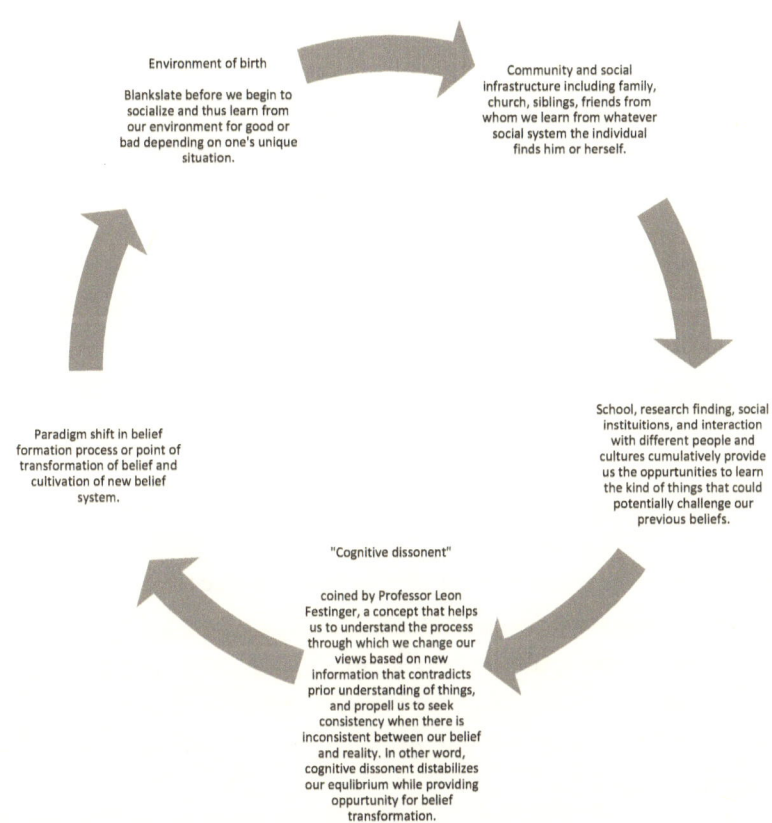

Environment of birth

Blankslate before we begin to socialize and thus learn from our environment for good or bad depending on one's unique situation.

Community and social infrastructure including family, church, siblings, friends from whom we learn from whatever social system the individual finds him or herself.

Paradigm shift in belief formation process or point of transformation of belief and cultivation of new belief system.

School, research finding, social instituitions, and interaction with different people and cultures cumulatively provide us the oppurtunities to learn the kind of things that could potentially challenge our previous beliefs.

"Cognitive dissonent"

coined by Professor Leon Festinger, a concept that helps us to understand the process through which we change our views based on new information that contradicts prior understanding of things, and propell us to seek consistency when there is inconsistent between our belief and reality. In other word, cognitive dissonent distabilizes our equlibrium while providing oppurtunity for belief transformation.

The above diagram demonstrates the process through which we accumulate experiences, values, and norms that interact and are infused into the formation of one's belief system. One's belief system is a function of the individual's collective internal and external experiences that include, among others, family, cultures, race, religion, gender, and ideation.

As stated previously, Mark Twain asserts, "Where you live really does shape who you are." Similarly, Ibn Khaldun, a North African Muslim scholar, reminds us that the rise or decline of human interaction with internal and external conditions combine to shape one's belief. Karl Marx echoed similar sentiment when he pointed out that men made their own history, but outside the condition of their choosing. I concur with the assertions by Twain, Khaldun, and Marx, especially when it comes to social issues, including those associated with gender bias.

Societal bias against women is demonstrated in almost all aspects of our lives – the social reproduction of the perception that women perform less than men seems to cement and sustain the notion, at least in the minds of some as supported in the Google incidents. We must be vigilant and ensure that such incidents are not treated in isolation. It is due to these accumulated experiences along with gender bias roles that society assigns to one's gender that has cumulatively shaped the view expressed by Google's engineer James Damore and the former president of Harvard University, Larry Summers.[34] None of these incidents happened in a vacuum. We are shaped by the company we keep; it suffices to conclude that both Larry Summers and Damore were shaped by experiences that amplified gender as a social construct.

Larry Summers and James Damore are united in their ideological position and contention that seems to be like a never-ending story of inequity women have endured generation after generation due to social constructs that stem from gender bias roles society assigns to people. The unfair roles that society places on people is a function of society's misconception that men outperform women based on real scientific evidence. This is a situation we can change through the belief transformation process, which is illustrated below.

---

[34] Goldenberg, Suzanne. 2005. Why women are poor at science, by Harvard president. *The Guardian*. https://www.theguardian.com/science/2005/jan/18/educationsgendergap.genderissues

Belief Transformation

As expressed above, belief transformation occurs when one is exposed to new information or experience that challenges one's earlier thoughts on a range of issues, such as gender, race, religion, and sexual orientation, among others. It is a process through which one questions earlier beliefs on issues and thus triggers what former Stanford University professor, Leon Festinger, characterized as cognitive dissonance.

Cognitive dissonance occurs when there is inconsistency between what we have known and new information we encounter. It's a process through which new information is introduced that forces one to change his or her earlier view to a new and more informed view on issues. With reference to gender, the societal role in shaping one's view is evinced and reflected in what one does. One's observed experiences, materials read, regardless of whether they were in the past or present, cumulatively shapes one's belief system. That belief system eventually influences how one behaves, as explained in previous chapters, particularly in Chapter Two.

In order to understand one's belief system, one must become familiar with the cultural values, biases, and institutions that cumulatively shape one's belief. Everyone's gets their belief system from their accumulated experiences. Each society or individual possesses specific cultural knowledge of his or her group; the specific knowledge and experiences combine to shape one's belief system. The same applies to gender and how societal culture pushes and reproduces the same when it comes to differential treatment based on one's gender. For one to truly understand other people, the individual must first analyze him or herself, by asking and honestly responding to the following questions:

i.   Who am I?

ii.   Why do I think or act the way I do – e.g. bias towards women?

iii. What factors influence my belief system?

To answer these important questions adequately, one must confront the questions honestly. It therefore requires one to begin by introspection and reflecting on his or her experiences from childhood. Reflect on shared values with friends, siblings, parents, and significant others. By doing so, one can then successfully conceptualize the origins of his or her gender belief system, and the relevancy to one's behavior and interpretation of reoccurring gender inequity and how those concepts influence one's view of gender.

Belief Formation Diagram.

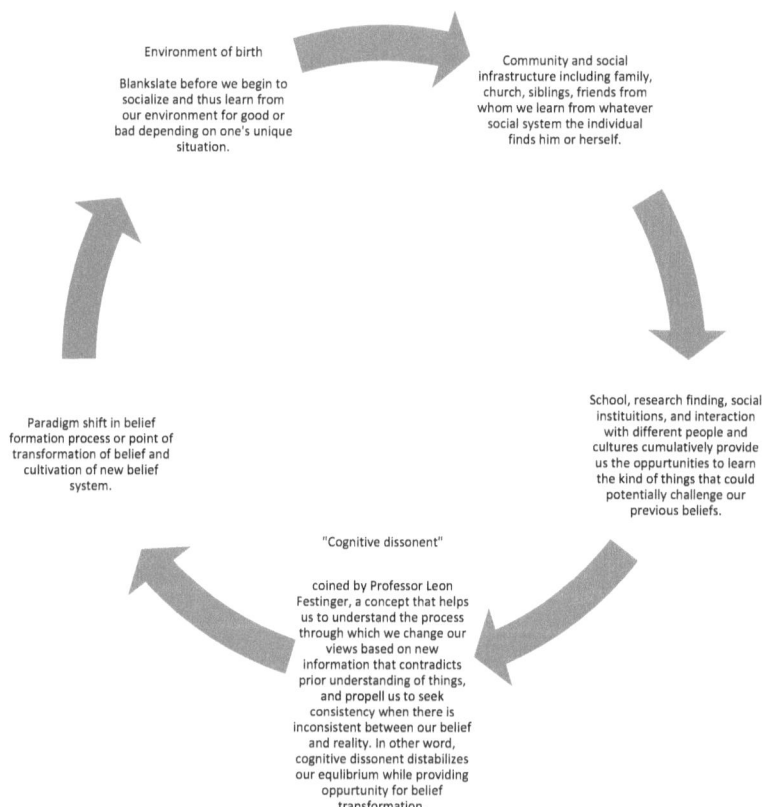

Environment of birth

Blankslate before we begin to socialize and thus learn from our environment for good or bad depending on one's unique situation.

Community and social infrastructure including family, church, siblings, friends from whom we learn from whatever social system the individual finds him or herself.

School, research finding, social institutions, and interaction with different people and cultures cumulatively provide us the oppurtunities to learn the kind of things that could potentially challenge our previous beliefs.

Paradigm shift in belief formation process or point of transformation of belief and cultivation of new belief system.

"Cognitive dissonent"

coined by Professor Leon Festinger, a concept that helps us to understand the process through which we change our views based on new information that contradicts prior understanding of things, and propell us to seek consistency when there is inconsistent between our belief and reality. In other word, cognitive dissonent distabilizes our equlibrium while providing oppurtunity for belief transformation.

One's observed experiences, materials read, good or bad, regardless of whether they were in the past or present, cumulatively continue to shape and influence one's belief system and how one behaves. Individuals or groups of people should pay attention to the construction of their belief system and what influenced that process.

As one examines these issues and how environmental factors interact to influence an individual's belief system, one gains a better and deeper understanding of the belief formation processes as illustrated above, and strategies for reversing, or in some cases, reconstruct one's belief system. Furthermore, we will explore the concept of belief formation based on several factors, such as culture, environment, social class, etc., and how one interacts with his/her cultural environment to nurture one's beliefs that ultimately drive one's behavior.

Gender issues remind us of the difficulties society has gone through, especially in the context of overt to covert discriminatory practices, and yet, generation after generation, we fail to address this issue. Therefore, the problems of gender inequity or racism and discrimination are still endemic in our society. Part of the reason why these problems persists is that good people stay silent when issues such as racism and gender discrimination occur. Unfortunately, this is despite the abundant nature of discrimination based on the issues associated with "isms," including gender and race that still bedevil us as a society. There are clearly not sufficient policies being espoused by leaders to put an end to discrimination in our society.

Despite the obvious marginalization of certain segments of our society on the basis of race or gender, etc., certain elements in our society are still in denial. This book provides insights into why, in spite our best efforts to eradicate racism, gender inequity, and others forms of discriminatory practices, we still have a long way to go in order to achieve equity and social justice, particularly in the relationship between black and white, minorities and some white police officers, women in executive positions in the workplace, just to mention a few.

Earlier, we demonstrated how one's beliefs can be changed through the process of a belief transformation process. This is a deliberate effort in which one goes through cognitive dissonance, the process through which one acquires new information that challenges one's accepted perception. With the advent of new information, one can employ the new information in order to cultivate a new belief that drives one's social and behavioral change.

As is often observed, gender prejudice usually stems from the bias a person forms based on experience. Often we hear, observe, or read about issues associated with gender prejudice, and the extent to which it humiliates not only the victims, but also their loved ones. Now that we have gained a better understanding of belief formation that drives all sorts of discriminatory practices, let's look at ways to address these issues from the organizational standpoint.

If you are a businessman or woman with a problem in sales, the first thing one would do is to establish an ad hoc committee to study the situation. Subsequently, they would come up with recommendations that they believe, if implemented properly, would lead to the eradication of the problems associated with sales.

Similarly, managers, whether men or women, should be aware of gender inequity. The issue is so ubiquitous in every aspect of our society that no one should miss it. Gender inequality comes in both overt as well as in covert forms. We should do what we can in order to combat gender bias and gender discrimination.

Secondly, organizations, regardless of whether they are public or private, must include policies that address the issues of gender inequity in their mission statements. The policies must unequivocally state equal pay for equal work; violence toward women will not be tolerated, and no more preference on who gets promoted based on gender. Similar statements build partnerships consisting of men and women of goodwill who are committed to fighting all types of gender inequity, regardless of what forms in which they come.

Thirdly, organizations, regardless of whether they are public or private, must provide regular training on gender responsive practices. The training must inform workers of the issues and behavior associated with gender equity. The policies and expected practices should be a guide for regular workshops and provide assessment metrics designed to measure improvements that will serve as the basis for further training while providing inspiration that propel members of the team to consistently strive for improvement with the belief that good is never enough where better is possible in their commitment to gender equity.

In the envisioned regular workshop trainings, the objectives and the outcome must be clearly defined and concisely stated. For example, if one is working on a workshop with the purpose of tackling gender inequity, one must clearly and unambiguously state the expected outcome of the workshop, such as:

By the end of each training session, participants will be able to:

- Define gender inequity in the context of their work, home, and their communities.
- Understand the organization's policies, procedures, and efforts necessary to provide equal opportunities to all regardless of one's gender or race or any of the issues associated with "isms."
- Explore and analyze individual perspectives on gender equity and continuously encourage discussions followed by debriefs on acceptable and unacceptable behaviors in the workplace and other areas of life.
- Develop handouts on gender responsive practices that are consistent with equality, social justice for all, and that support organizational mission.

In conclusion, I believe that the only way to tackle the gender inequity in our society is to employ more aggressive and comprehensive policies that address gender equity issues. In addition, we need to cultivate a culture of effective communication that promotes mutual respect and harmonious relationships among the genders. Organizational leadership must commit to continuously train employees on issues related to gender equity. With an open exchange of ideas, perhaps participants will become conversant with issues associated with gender equity in its complex forms, not just from their individual perspectives, but also from the organization's perspective that would inevitably foster necessary change on our societal misconception and marginalization of women. I believe that with open exchange, participants in conferences and other engagement-driven activities, they will be encouraged to develop a road map for understanding issues of inequity, and ultimately, benefit from the huge advantage of inclusivity in our society and elsewhere.

REFLECTION ON THE CHAPTER

As you finish reading the chapter, please reflect on how it resonates with you in the context of your past, present, and how the future looks. Please consider the past and your present experience as you proceed. As you think through those experiences, be specific as to how the chapter relates to your unique experience. Try to connect some of what you read to your own experience or the experience of other people that you know.

_____

_____

_____

_____

_____

_____

_____

If you were able to relate or make connections, based on those connections you made, in what ways would you relay such powerful information to provide learning opportunities to others, especially young people?

_____

_____

_____

_____

_____

_____

_____

In what ways has the content of this chapter helped you to ignite your metacognition while linking those experiences to multitudes of other experiences? As you reflect, please discuss how your experiences help foster meaningful understanding of the issues from one or more perspectives.

_____

_____

_____

_____

_____

_____

If you have no relatable experience, please feel free to express that too. The aim of this chapter is to keep engaging with one another in exploring these issues. We cannot solve these issues by isolating them or pretending that they don't happen.

_____

_____

_____

_____

_____

_____

CHAPTER 5

SEXUAL HARASSMENT IN THE WORKPLACE

The recent overwhelming allegations of sexual harassment by those in powerful positions has stunned the nation and the world in general. This has prompted so many people to question "What is sexual harassment?" The Civil Rights Act of 1964 came close to answering the above question, but it did not go far enough. At best, sexual harassment is only ambiguously interpreted. There is certainly no clear definition of what constitutes sexual harassment in today's interpretation. The definition of sexual harassment mainly focuses on employment discriminatory practices based on one's gender.

The United States Equal Employment Opportunity Commission (EEOC) defines sexual harassment as follows: "It is unlawful to harass a person (an applicant or employee) because of that person's sex."[35] The EEOC's focus in 1965 was essentially on issues of application and employee discriminatory practices that were widespread at the time. Therefore, the 1965 law was neither enough nor specific enough and that may explain sustained sexual harassment as it has been exposed by current and trending allegations of sexual misconduct, especially by those in positions of power. It should have been clearer and perhaps the definition should have been explained more precisely by including that it is also "the act of bullying or coercion

---

[35] Berg, Richard K. "Equal employment opportunity under the Civil Rights Act of 1964." Brook. L. Rev. 31 (1964): 62.

of a sexual nature, or the unwelcome or inappropriate promise of rewards in exchange for sexual favors" as observed in recent misbehaviors of those in powerful positions in several organizations, including the United States Congress.

The Civil Rights Act of 1964 provided that "It is unlawful to harass a person (an applicant or employee)." However, this explanation has been enhanced through the development of case laws, such as the amendment in 2005 that provided two clear definitions of sexual harassment. Sexual harassment goes beyond our nation's boundary. It also happens in other countries around the world and most countries like us are trying to do something about it. Great Britain, for example, has advanced laws to tackle sexual harassment, such as the Sex Discrimination Act 1975 (c. 65), an Act of the Parliament of the United Kingdom, which protects men and women from discrimination on the grounds of sex or marital status. Furthermore, the amendment of Sexual Discrimination Act in 2005 introduced two clear definitions of sexual harassment: "Unwanted conduct on the grounds of someone's sex; and unwanted physical, verbal or non-verbal conduct of a sexual nature." Additionally, the European Parliament has defined "harassment related to sex" as:

> "Where an unwanted conduct related to the sex of a person occurs with the purpose or effect of violating the dignity of a person, and of creating an intimidating, hostile, degrading, humiliating or offensive environment."[36]

The combination of 2005 developmental case law and the European Parliament harassment laws provides a more inclusive definition of sexual harassment with less ambiguities. It may have provided an even better definition of sexual harassment and may very well explain the upward swing in reporting of sexual harassment and abuse observed today.

Some have argued that sexual harassment is not on the upward swing, but rather that people are now more open about reporting instance of sexual

---

[36] EUR-Lex. Retrieved from https://eur-lex.europa.eu/legal-content/EN/ALL/?uri=URISERV:c10940

harassment, as witnessed in the increased number of sexual harassment charges against well-known individuals. These were the types of stories that were unheard of because the people in power that perpetuate such oppressive acts often threaten their victims to stay in silence. Now with the support of media and increased freedom, victims feel safe to speak out.

For instance, former judge and Alabama senate candidate, Roy Moore, had been accused of perpetuating or engaging in activities that suggest he was involved in numerous sexual harassment cases involving women, even with underage children. Incidentally, Judge Moore was accused only recently of these repeated acts. It seems that people are now more emboldened and encouraged to report sexual harassment that they experienced in the past. Currently, at this writing, the number of women accusing Judge Moore of sexual harassment has drastically risen to nine women.[37]

This clearly suggests that since the advent of metoo (#Metoo), more and more victims of sexual harassment are emboldened, and they are courageously coming forward and reporting what they have endured. A *Miami Herald* writer asserts, "A decade before MeToo, a multimillionaire sex offender from Florida got the ultimate break."[38] She further reported about Jeffrey Epstein's alleged harassment acts. According to the police in a Palm Beach town, Jeffrey Epstein repeatedly engaged in sexual activity with underage girls at his waterfront Palm Beach home on El Brillo Way. Epstein also owns residences in New York City and the U.S. Virgin Islands, among other locales.[39] In that piece, *Miami Herald* investigative reporter Julie K. Brown asserts that "As the #MeToo movement spurred a national conversation about the sexual harassment and abuse of women, the *Miami Herald* had already begun examining the Jeffrey Epstein case."

[37] Cooney, Samantha. 2017. More Women Are Accusing Roy Moore of Sexual Misconduct. Here's Everything You Need to Know About the Scandal. Time.Com. http://time.com/5029172/roy-moore-accusers/

[38] Brown, Julie. & Albright Aaron. 2018. Perversion of Justice. *Miami Herald*. https://www.miamiherald.com/news/local/article221897990.html

[39] Brown, Julie. 2018. "Cops worked to put serial sex abuser in prison. Prosecutors worked to cut him a break". *Miamiherald.com*. https://www.miamiherald.com/news/local/article214210674.html

Ms. Brown further reflected on what her investigation was uncovering and revealing allegations linking people in powerful positions, including the former Miami U.S. Attorney Alexander Acosta and his role in helping to orchestrate a secret plea bargain in which the prosecutors struck a deal to end Epstein's sexual harassment of teenage children case. Ms. Brown also described a disturbing experience that a victim went through in the hands of the perpetrator. The victim explained that "A silver-haired man wearing nothing but a white towel came into the room. He lay face down on a massage table, and while talking on a phone, directed Licata to rub his back, legs, and feet." These are the kind of things kids are subjected to and victimizers go unpunished and victims are shamed for. Thanks to the #MeToo Movement, sexual harassment has been exposed as a crime while emboldening and encouraging the victims to fight back.

Obviously, the current sexual harassment uptick is a result of the new openness in reporting as compared to the past when it was taboo, and victims were threatened, silenced, and ashamed to the extent that no victim would be willing to identify him or herself. This is also the case in both public and private organizations, especially in a work environment, where perpetrators are usually in a position of power. No one seems to be willing to challenge or upend their prospects for promotion or an increase in salary or stature by powerful individuals. There is an unprecedented increase in reports of sexual harassment since the birth of the #MeToo movement.

As mentioned, Judge Roy Moore's recent alleged incidents of sexual harassment has led to calls for him to step down, especially by members of his own party, including the Senate Majority Leader, Mitch McConnell, and the then Speaker of the House, Paul Ryan, among others.[40] In November 2017, there was an explosive revelation that Senator Al Franken groped and forcefully kissed a woman without her consent during an overseas USO tour in 2006. This incident happened two years prior to Franken's senatorial election victory. The victim, Leeann Tweeden, a news anchor on TalkRadio 790 KABC in Los Angeles, posted her story on the

---

[40] Cooney, Samantha. 2017. More Women Are Accusing Roy Moore of Sexual Misconduct. Here's Everything You Need to Know About the Scandal. Time.Com. http://time.com/5029172/roy-moore-accusers/

station's website. In her statement to the perpetrator (Sen. Al Franken) and the public, she stated, "You knew exactly what you were doing." She continued, "You forcibly kissed me without my consent, grabbed my breasts while I was sleeping, and had someone take a photo of you doing it, knowing I would see it later and be ashamed."[41]

In response to her accusation, Senator Al Franken apologized clearly and concisely without equivocation, asserting that he was wrong, which makes him different from other politicians accused of sexual harassment. Even the President of the United States, Donald Trump, has been allegedly accused of sexual harassment and abuse by several women.

Following recent high-profile reports by the media and subsequent meaningful blow-back on sexual harassment and new exposure to the issue, the fact that remains that the workplace is more diverse now than any time in our history. This may be a contributing factor to a renewed focus on sexual harassment and the subsequent shift on how sexual harassment is perceived and treated. There is clearly a litany of reported sexual harassment charges perpetuated by those in powerful positions towards people in less powerful positions, and mostly against women. In fact, it is so common in our corporate culture that one has to be blind not to see it.

Some of the most recent high-profile sexual harassment allegations that continue to trend as I write this piece are the Bill Cosby, Bill O'Reilly, and Harvey Weinstein scandals, all of whom the press allege "paid off sexual harassment accusers for decades."[42] Besides the above famous people, a spate of allegations had been made against numerous other powerful men, especially those in the film industry and media, including director James Toback, director Brett Ratner, and many others, with new allegations

---

[41] Wong, Herman. 2017. 'Where do his hands go?' Trump takes aim at 'Al Frankenstein' over groping claims. Washingtonpost.Com. https://www.washingtonpost.com/news/politics/wp/2017/11/16/trump-takes-aim-at-al-franken-over-groping-claims/?utm_term=.f7060b401e48

[42] Kantor, Jodi and Twohey, Megan. 2017. Harvey Weinstein Paid Off Sexual Harassment Accusers for Decades. NYTimes. https://www.nytimes.com/2017/10/05/us/harvey-weinstein-harassment-allegations.html

being brought to light every day.[43] In fact, more claims are surfacing in almost every industry, including one in which a Boston media official alleged that her son was sexually harassed and embarrassed by a famous actor, Kevin Spacey.

Even with the numerous high-profile sexual harassments allegations, I'm unable to decide which allegation to focus on first, because there are so many and they all possess some common attributes and yet are different in the sense that there is now a change in the way sexual harassments are handled. Clearly, there is a big change in how sexual harassment is handled now than in the past where victims were often afraid to come forward.

In the past, perpetrators of sexual harassment used their powerful position to harass and subsequently subject victims to sexual and emotional anguish, and above all, they were never held accountable. This situation had occurred repeatedly where victims were usually subordinates, in less powerful positions and thus insecure to openly discuss their sexual harassment experience. That in part explains why the so-called powerful abusers and sexual harassers got away with their behaviors, behaviors that by and large went unpunished because witnesses and victims remained silent.

Today, there seems to be change in how sexual harassment is conceptualized. The entire society is finally opening their eyes to what sexual harassment victims endure. Therefore, members of our society are strongly against the perpetrators, who usually have significant power and use it to manipulate their less powerful and insecure subordinates into submission, sometimes threatening their victims into silence. There is a big difference in how we perceive and treat sexual harassment and we can further explain this phenomenon via belief formation processes as presented below.

---

[43] Rhian, Daly. 2017. Uma Thurman says she's 'waiting to feel less angry' before discussing sexual harassment in Hollywood. https://www.nme.com/news/film/uma-thurman-says-shes-waiting-feel-less-angry-discussing-sexual-harassment-hollywood-2156522

Belief Transformation Diagram on Sexual Harassment

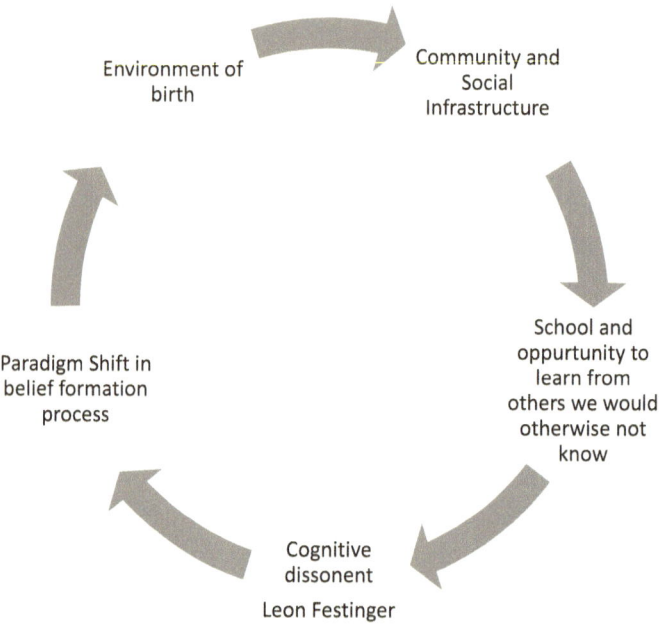

In her piece in the *Washington Times*, Thursday, November 2, 2017, Valerie Richardson exposed the dark secret of sexual harassment in both liberal and conservative media.[44] Furthermore, she reminded people that this is neither a Democratic nor Republican issue; it is an American issue, which she substantiated this way,

> "Five months ago, the *New Republic* rebuked Fox News for its 'toxic workplace for women,' citing sexual misconduct accusations against former chief Roger Ailes. It turns out that the same thing could have been said of the *New Republic*."

She continued,

---

[44] Richardson, Valerie. 2017. The Washington Times. 'Year of the Woman' senators condemn sexual harassment, campaigned for Ted Kennedy. https://www.washingtontimes.com/news/2017/nov/19/patty-murray-campaigned-ted-kennedy-after-decrying/

"Two of the liberal magazine's most prominent figures have been accused of sexual harassment as aftershocks from the Harvey Weinstein scandal reverberate through some of the nation's leading journalism outlets. Those include ABC, NBC, MSNBC, the *New York Times*, National Public Radio, and Vox Media — left-tilting outlets that have become vulnerable to charges of hypocrisy for championing women in public while apparently tolerating or failing to notice offensive behavior in their newsrooms."

Besides the above, Valarie continued,

"There's hubbub surrounding a list, first revealed last month by BuzzFeed, an anonymous spreadsheet making the rounds that reportedly lists dozens of men accused of offenses including physical violence, 'flirting' and 'weird lunch dates.'"

She further stated,

"Journalism isn't the only industry rocked by the 'Weinstein effect,' but the sheer number of high-profile newsmen accused of sexual misconduct has insiders waiting to see whose name will next surface on the wrong side of a headline."

Clearly, it seems that as one episode of sexual harassment ends, another begins. It is like a never-ending story that continuously fuels the cultivation of sexual harassment in our society. Sexual harassment, as difficult and complex issue that it is, it's often denied by some and simplified by others, which cumulatively continues to contribute to the creation of a culture of even bigger sexual harassment issue in our society.

The question then becomes, why is it that despite public concern about sexual harassment, why is it still prevalent? What are the factors fostering sexual harassment in our society? What can be done to eradicate the culture that allows sexual harassment against women and transform our society from the one that appears to condone sexual harassment to one that is free of sexual harassment? The answers to the above questions are vital to addressing sexual harassment in our society.

Before we can dive into the above questions, let's explore what causes and sustains sexual harassment. As we have been clear from the beginning of this book, one's belief system is the core driver of the individual's behavior, and that remains the case when it comes to the issue of sexual harassment and subjugation of women to second-class citizens. In order to grasp this issue, exploring and understanding the process of belief formation that drives and sustains sexual harassment is important. As we had stated earlier, one's belief system is by and large the function of the individual's experience, environment, culture, values, and institutions such as religious affiliation among others as illustrated by the diagram below:

Belief Formation Diagram

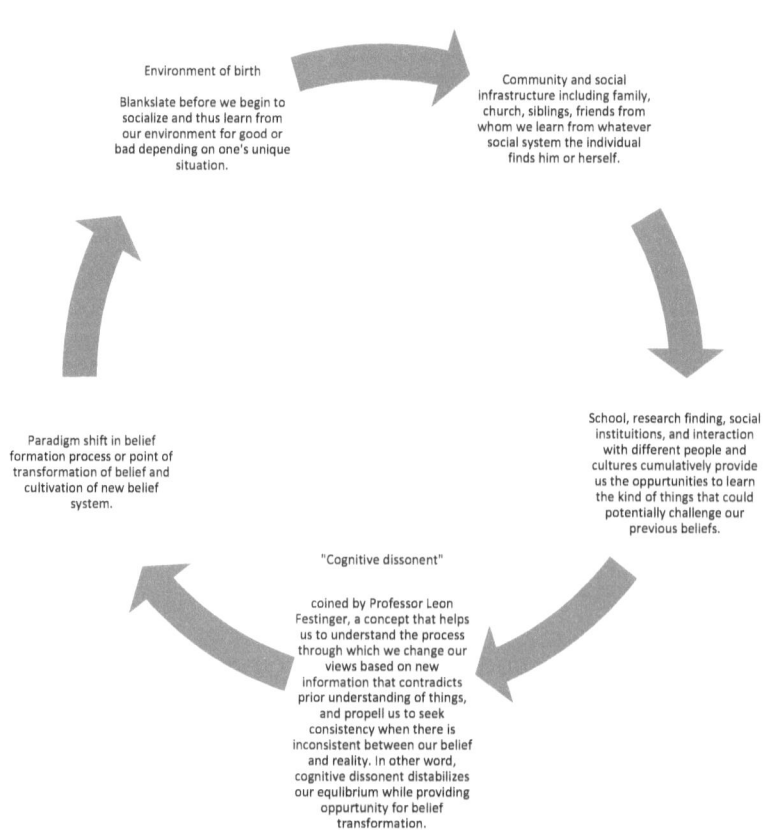

Environment of birth

Blankslate before we begin to socialize and thus learn from our environment for good or bad depending on one's unique situation.

Community and social infrastructure including family, church, siblings, friends from whom we learn from whatever social system the individual finds him or herself.

School, research finding, social instituitions, and interaction with different people and cultures cumulatively provide us the oppurtunities to learn the kind of things that could potentially challenge our previous beliefs.

Paradigm shift in belief formation process or point of transformation of belief and cultivation of new belief system.

"Cognitive dissonent"

coined by Professor Leon Festinger, a concept that helps us to understand the process through which we change our views based on new information that contradicts prior understanding of things, and propel us to seek consistency when there is inconsistent between our belief and reality. In other word, cognitive dissonent destabilizes our equlibrium while providing oppurtunity for belief transformation.

The above diagram demonstrates the process through which we accumulate experiences, values, and norms that interact and infuse into the formation of one's belief system, and the same process repeats itself when it comes to sexual harassment. Sexual harassment stems from evidence of sexual and social roles society places on people based upon their harassment experiences. Sexual harassment is a social construct, usually stemming from people in positions of power. Some of these acts are driven by the roles the society assigns to people based on their genders and their position of power and how they are supposed to act in sexual harassment cases. The unfair roles that society places on people is a function of the society's misconception that men could harass women sexually and socially thus engage in reproduction of the perception that powerful people in leadership positions could perpetuate sexual harassment and still get away with it, and that encourages them to do it over and over and again.

Belief Transformation

In fact, I have argued elsewhere that exposure to different viewpoints is the mother of invention. For instance, in modern business, people have associated conflict with innovation as "Disruptive Innovation." Innovation that could lead to the creation of new markets, gaining new market shares or changing views as a result of new research. Disruptive Innovation or Disruptive Technology can be seen in the advent of new technologies like the home computer, the cell phone, or the High Definition (flat screen) Television (HDTV). These three Disruptive Technologies have changed how we live and how we do business today.

In an earlier chapter, we discussed how "Disruptive Technology" provides avenues for new and innovative ideas. Basically, belief transformation stems from the acquisition of new knowledge that challenges old paradigms or old perspectives and provides the framework for new perspectives or changes in attitude, and by extension, behavior. Can you imagine what the world would be like without personal computers, the internet, cell phones, or HDTV? The same is true in any paradigm shift, including the issue of sexual harassment.

As we can see, exposure to sexual harassment by the perpetuators cumulatively results in better information currently being shared about sexual harassment, unlike in the past, when sexual harassment was denied, and, in some ways, victimizers were helped to sustain sexual harassment, considering how sexual harassment was punished or rewarded in our society. As expressed above, belief transformation occurs when one is exposed to new information or experience that contradicts one's earlier thought on a range of issues such as sexual harassment.

Again, belief transformation occurs when one questions earlier beliefs on issues and thus triggers that process of cognitive dissonance, the process through which new information is introduced and this information has the potential to propel one to change his or her earlier view to a new and more informed view on an issue, in this case, sexual harassment. As the recent exposure of the powerful and their alleged sexual harassment deeds, the humiliation and legal punishment among others are cumulatively facilitating new openness and a new understanding of the humiliation, pain and anguish associated with sexual harassment. It's bringing people to a new understanding of what victims go through and the pain they bear, introducing a change in how sexual harassment is perceived and dealt with in our society.

In addition, victims are speaking out against sexual harassment, thus giving other people a chance of vocalizing their opinions against sexual harassers. These emotional roles referenced above on sexual harassment are triggering a change in the societal role in shaping one's view on sexual harassment. Recent observation on sexual harassment as documented by Valerie Richardson on Thursday, November 2, 2017 is clearly supporting the notion of a social shift on sexual harassment.[45] In addition, what had previously been taboo, where victims were afraid of reporting harassment, has since changed. Prominent celebrities who were either afraid to report or others who remained silent are speaking out and calling sexual harassment what it ought to be called, "criminal," and criticize those who engage in the practice. Clearly, that

---

[45] Richardson, Valerie. 2017. 'Year of the Woman' senators condemn sexual harassment, campaigned for Ted Kennedy. *The Washington Times*. https://www.washingtontimes.com/news/2017/nov/19/patty-murray-campaigned-ted-kennedy-after-decrying/

is a transformation of our belief system that will inevitably shame the perpetrators of sexual harassment and ultimately eradicate the practice of sexual harassment from our social and workplace cultures.

Since it was established in 1965, the Equal Employment Opportunities Commission (EEOC) has been concerned about sexual harassment in the workplace. Over the years, the Commission has used its powers under the 1975 Sex Discrimination Act (SDA) to investigate claims of sexual harassment at employment tribunals, to develop case law, and has raised awareness of the problem through campaigns and lobbying. The EEOC has also prompted investigation of organizations that have a high number of sexual harassment complaints. This inappropriate act has been going on for too long, even in the heart of our nation's capital. The U.S. Congress is now investigating this issue. In fact, some congressional employees have also reported their own sexual harassment experiences in the hands of their male counterparts. Congress seems to be speaking out on the need for a change when it comes to addressing the issue of sexual harassment. This change is precipitating action to prevent future harassment in workplaces, including in the United States Congress, which is considering new legislation to fight sexual harassment throughout the country.

Now that we have gained a better understanding of belief formation that drives human and societal behaviors, including on issues associated with sexual harassment, let's look at ways to address these issues from the organizational standpoint. For example, if you are associated with a business where there is evidence of sexual harassment, and it's affecting the most important resource of the organization, human resources, and perhaps by extension, it's affecting other aspects of the business operation. Clearly, this issue needs to be addressed by the leadership. The point of contention is what those in leadership can do to address the problem. As mentioned previously, if you are a businessman or in leadership position, the first thing to do is establish an ad hoc committee to study the situation with a focus on sexual harassment. Subsequently, they would come up with recommendations that they believe, if implemented properly, would lead to the eradication of sexual harassment in the organization. It should be also made clear so that everyone knows exactly what constitutes sexual harassment and the consequences for anyone who engages in any acts that fits into what constitutes sexual harassment regardless of one's position. It should also be clear that the organization won't tolerate any form of sexual harassment regardless of whether it comes in overt or covert forms and the leadership will take every measure to combat sexual harassment in the organization.

Regardless of whether they are public or private, small or big, organizations must include policies that address the issues of sexual harassment in their mission statements. The policies must precisely state: the organization's commitment to zero tolerance of sexual harassment acts toward anyone, men or women. There should be regular training on issues of sexual harassment, practices that must be aligned and stated clearly in the organization's policy statement. The training must consistently educate participants to be familiar with information. Participants need to learn what they can do to address the issues associated with sexual harassment and personal responsibilities as well as those that involve others so as to engage in best practices. Organizations should always be proactive in preventing activities that could potentially lead to sexual harassment and instead support those activities that encourage members of the team to consistently strive for improvement with the belief that good is never enough where better is possible in their quest to discourage any act of sexual harassment.

In the envisioned regular workshop trainings, the objectives and the outcome must be clearly defined and concisely stated. For example, if one is working on a workshop with the purpose of preventing sexual harassment activities, one must clearly and unambiguously state the expected outcome of the workshop, such as;

By the end of each training session, participants will be able to:

- Define sexual harassment in context of their work environment.
- Understand the organization's policies, procedures, and efforts necessary to prevent sexual harassment in the organization.
- Develop handouts on sexual harassment in ways that are consistent with equality, social justice for all, and in ways that support the organization's mission.

In conclusion, I believe that the only way to tackle sexual harassment in our society is to employ more aggressive and comprehensive policies that address sexual harassment issues in the mission statement. In addition, cultivate a culture of effective communication that promotes mutual respect and harmonious relationships among people in the organization. Organizational leadership must commit to continuously train employees on issues related to sexual harassment and issues of equity. With an open exchange of ideas, perhaps participants will become conversant with issues associated with sexual harassment in its complex forms, not just from their individual perspectives, but also from the organization's perspective. I believe that with open exchange, participants in conferences and other engagement will engage in activities that are designed to address sexual harassment issues while developing a road map for understanding issues and ultimately benefit from being informed about sexual harassment.

REFLECTION ON THE CHAPTER

As you finish reading the chapter, please reflect on how it resonates with you in the context of your past, present, and how the future looks. Please consider the past and your present experience as you proceed. As you think through those experiences, be specific as to how the chapter relates to your unique experience. Try to connect some of what you read to your own experience or the experience of other people that you know.

_____

_____

_____

_____

_____

_____

_____

If you were able to relate or make connections, based on those connections you made, in what ways would you relay such powerful information to provide learning opportunities to others, especially young people?

_____

_____

_____

_____

_____

_____

_____

In what ways has the content of this chapter helped you to ignite your metacognition while linking those experiences to multitudes of other experiences? As you reflect, please discuss how your experiences help foster meaningful understanding of the issues from one or more perspectives.

If you have no relatable experience, please feel free to express that too. The aim of this chapter is to keep engaging with one another in exploring these issues. We cannot solve these issues by isolating them or pretending that they don't happen.

CHAPTER 6

ON RACE, RACIST BELIEF FORMATION AND NECESSARY TRANSFORMATION TO PERFECT THE ENVISIONED UNION

Every day, we come across behaviors motivated by racist acts. In recent years, there has been a steady increase in hate-related acts around the country. Some of these incidents are deadly with frighteningly high frequency. The most recent tragic incidents include the incident in Pittsburgh in which eleven American Jews were shot and killed in their synagogue.[46] These acts are driven by hate and often take place in the form of white supremacists targeting those different from them, as in the case of the two African Americans shot and killed after the alleged assailant attempted and failed to enter a predominantly African American church.[47]

---

[46] Campbell, Robertson., Mele, Christopher,. & Tavernise, Sabrina. 2018. 11 Killed in Synagogue Massacre; Suspect Charged With 29 Counts. *The New York Times.* https://www.nytimes.com/2018/10/27/us/active-shooter-pittsburgh-synagogue-shooting.html

[47] Karimi, Faith. 2018. Man who killed 2 at Kroger tried to enter a predominantly black church minutes earlier, police say. *CNN.* https://edition.cnn.com/2018/10/26/us/kentucky-kroger-shooting/index.html

Racially motivated acts are becoming rampant in our society. Another incident occurred in Charleston, South Carolina. This incident raised the consciousness of the entire nation when a twenty-one-year-old white supremacist (a person who believes that they are only superior because of their white race) who claimed that he wanted to start a race war walked into a gathering of churchgoers and proceeded to fire a weapon, killing nine parishioners. Dylann Roof, a self-proclaimed white supremacist, entered the Emanuel African Methodist Episcopal church in Charleston and killed innocent parishioners. Politicians and citizens alike expressed their outrage and concern over what happened in Charleston.[48]

In similar but through more organized channels, groups with similar ideologies design ways to frighten, intimidate, and sometimes kill people simply because they are different from them. Included in these groups are white supremacist, white nationalist, and neo-Nazi hate groups. The groups gathered together in Charlottesville, Virginia to spew hate and spread their racist ideologies during the "Unite the Right Rally." They made headlines in national newspapers, televised news programs, and social media. These racist groups are people who believe that they are not only superior to those they victimize, but that they have the right to destroy lives. The impact of hate in our society was also viewed in Charlottesville, Virginia when a twenty-year-old white man drove his car into a sea of (mostly white) people at an anti-fascist rally, killing one protestor and injuring thirteen others. The protestors were at a counter-protest against the white supremacist "Unite the Right" rally that was also being held in Charlottesville.

Charlottesville's racist incident took the life of a courageous white woman named Heather Heyer. Although the advocates of equity and social justice appear to have lost a champion, Heather unquestionably still continues to inspire others. In my view, I see Heather Heyer as a leader who stood

---

[48] Associated Press (AP). 2016. Dylann Roof's confession shown to jury at Charleston church shooting trial. *CBS News.* https://www.cbsnews.com/news/dylann-roof-confession-fbi-jury-charleston-church-shooting-trial/

up and courageously advocated for equity and social justice for all.[49] May her gentle soul rest in peace, along with others with whom she shared the same belief of equity and social justice for all, including former Attorney General of the United States, Bobby Kennedy, and Civil Rights icon, Dr. Martin Luther King, Jr.

As Heather's mother, Susan Bro, said, "They tried to kill my child to shut her up, but guess what, you just magnified her." It was reported that Ms. Bro's comment sparked an ovation from a packed theater in downtown Charlottesville that lasted nearly a minute and a half. It was done to honor a committed equity and social justice champion and Heather's mother, Ms. Bro. Clearly, Heather's legacy will leave and serve as a source of inspiration for standing up and courageously challenging hate and evil in all its forms.[50]

Although both Charleston and Charlottesville raised the issue of race and racism to the conscience of our nation, these incidences are not isolated acts. They are simply endemic of the numerous racist-driven acts that have occurred and continue to occur in the United States and around the world. These incidences of racist behavior are difficult and complex to explain. They are denied by some and over-simplified by others, which cumulatively continues to fuel these incidences in different magnitudes within our society. But these visible and very public acts of racism are not the core of how racism spreads through society.

---

[49] Silverman, Ellie, Hernández Arelis & Hendrix, Steve. 2017. They tried to kill my child to shut her up,' Heather Heyer's mother mourns at funeral for woman killed during Nazi protest in Charlottesville. Washingtonpost.Com https://www.washingtonpost.com/local/heather-heyers-grieving-mother-readies-herself-for-huge-public-farewell-to-my-child/2017/08/15/c5270e5e-81fa-11e7-ab27-1a21a8e006ab_story.html

[50] Silverman, Ellie., Hernández Arelis & Hendrix, Steve. 2017. They tried to kill my child to shut her up,' Heather Heyer's mother mourns at funeral for woman killed during Nazi protest in Charlottesville. Washingtonpost.Com https://www.washingtonpost.com/local/heather-heyers-grieving-mother-readies-herself-for-huge-public-farewell-to-my-child/2017/08/15/c5270e5e-81fa-11e7-ab27-1a21a8e006ab_story.html

While the visible and noticeable racist acts are in form of direct verbal and physical actions that are recognizable because they are "in your face," a larger problem in our society is the less direct, or covert racism that also persists. Most of us have a dual persona, one that is visible and one that is internal and not that visible (inner core). The invisible persona is only known to the individual and can often be effectively concealed.

Covert racism is part of one's inner core and known only to the individual that has it. In fact, the perpetrators of this type of racist thoughts/behaviors are cowards; they strive to conceal their nefarious behaviors. They do not want their secret acts to be made public, and unfortunately, they successfully keep these thoughts/behaviors under wraps, like Robert Bowers, who never did anything to indicate the hate in him, except the anti-Semitic statements he reportedly made during the shooting and targeted Jews on social media, according to a federal law enforcement official.[51]

The Visible or "In Your Face" Racist Acts

Visible racist actors are those who perpetuate the kind of pain that can be characterized as "in your face" blatant racist behaviors. These are the kind of racist acts that are bold and often defiantly aggressive. The perpetrators of this magnitude of racist acts have no qualms inflicting maximum causalities in the open as seen in several places, including at a synagogue in Pittsburgh, Pennsylvania, and Charlottesville, Virginia and Charleston, South Carolina, where the perpetrator, Dylann Roof, wasted no time confessing having massacred nine innocent victims at Emanuel African Methodist Episcopal church. He confidently stated in a videotaped confession to police, "I went to that church in Charleston and, uh, I did it," while laughing.[52]

---

[51] Campbell, Robertson., Mele, Christopher,. & Tavernise, Sabrina. 2018. 11 Killed in Synagogue Massacre; Suspect Charged With 29 Counts. *The New York Times*. https://www.nytimes.com/2018/10/27/us/active-shooter-pittsburgh-synagogue-shooting.html

[52] Associated Press (AP). 2016. Dylann Roof's confession shown to jury at Charleston church shooting trial. *CBS News*. https://www.cbsnews.com/news/dylann-roof-confession-fbi-jury-charleston-church-shooting-trial/

In fact, that is their main purpose, to be noticed. They want to be known and feared by all, especially their victims, as proven in racist acts coordinated and executed in Charlottesville and Charleston. The incident in Charlottesville especially is a clear illustration of what an evil act of racism entails.

The Invisible, Subtle, or Covert Racist Acts

Covert racism is carried out by those who understand that most of the people would not buy into their racist ideas, and thus, they learn how to conceal their racist behaviors. They carry out more sophisticated types of racist acts surreptitiously. This is the type of racist behavior that the perpetrators strive to hide. They know that exposure of their wrongdoings would create a bad image and bring shame upon them. These are the kind of racist behaviors that are subtle and mainly occur in professional job discrimination or promotional practices where victims are denied opportunities for jobs and promotions by some. The perpetrators of covert racism subversively act as if they do not know what they are doing, but, in fact, they do.

For example, there has been evidence that some politicians use their power to neutralize the strength of minority voters, or intentionally create artificial hurdles to impede their victims' ability to vote in elections while giving an advantage to those who would vote in their favor. An instance of this occurred in Pennsylvania, according to *Washington Post* reporter Aaron Blake.[53] There are other nefarious ways through which discrimination plays in political arenas by those who simply create institutional and personal obstacles in our democratic process that come in the form of gerrymandering, voter suppression, and an avalanche of lobbyists who focus on what is good for them rather than what is good for the country.

This is an issue Dr. Martin Luther King fought for along with other civil rights advocates in the 1960s. The fight for fair voting rights is still going

---

[53] Blake, Aaron. 2012. "Republicans Keep Admitting That Voter ID Helps Them Win, For Some Reason". *Tinyurl.Com*. https://tinyurl.com/ycm7ldfy.

on in now, against another type of racist act where the perpetrators are deceptively creating structural impediments to prevent certain segments of our populations from exercising their voting rights; it's like the poll taxes all over again. We also see this soft bigotry and racist-driven acts in our criminal justice system, where some police departments have been documented for their nefarious and differential mistreatment of minorities as well as other aspects of our criminal justice system as confirmed in a Department of Justice investigation of the disproportionate mistreatment of minorities in all three cities where the investigations took place: Ferguson, Missouri; Baltimore, Maryland; and Chicago, Illinois, a sentiment Michelle Alexander captured well in her book, *The New Jim Crow*.[54]

In order to ascertain what influences racist behavior, we have to analyze the answer to the question "What is it that cultivates and nurtures the racist belief system?" We have repurposed the above question to enable one to find what influences racist thoughts/behaviors, and more importantly, what propels people to act in a racist manner? And perhaps we can find solutions to permanently address the issue of race and racism through belief transformation, an issue that will be explored in a moment; but before we get to that, let's focus on the belief formation that drives race and racist acts.

Racist Belief Formation Process

In Chapters Two and Three, we explored the belief formation process. It has clearly become the center of focus and crucial for one to gain a deeper understanding of the process that results in the cultivation of racist views. No one was born to hate; it's all socially constructed ideas that ultimately propel people to act in a racist manner.

Research has demonstrated that hate is a socially constructed act. The process of belief transformation provides the road map for racists to transform and evolve beyond racist thoughts, as shown in Derek's case. Derek was one of those who cultivated and nurtured a racist-driven belief

---

[54] Alexander, Michelle. "The New Jim Crow." Ohio St. J. Crim. L. 9 (2011): 7.

system but eventually transformed through engagement with people he did not know, but people who courageously confronted him and ultimately helped him transform his racist belief system to a non-racist one.

Belief formation and what informs one's behavior as an individuals or group.

What informs one's belief system? Why does one's belief system propel him or her to do what he or she does, including being potentially a racist and a killer, for that matter? Those are some of the questions that are going to be explored in the remaining part of this chapter with a focus on race. This is in turn impacted the individual or group's behaviors.

Central to human behavior is one's belief system. One's belief system is the core driver of the individual's behavior; this remains the case regardless of whether it is a good or bad behavior. Racist acts are a function of one's belief system. Let us spend some time to explore and understand the process of racial belief formation, which is shaped by one's experience, culture, values, and in some cases, social institutions such as schools and churches, as will be demonstrated momentarily.

Belief Formation Process: Illustrated in Diagram.

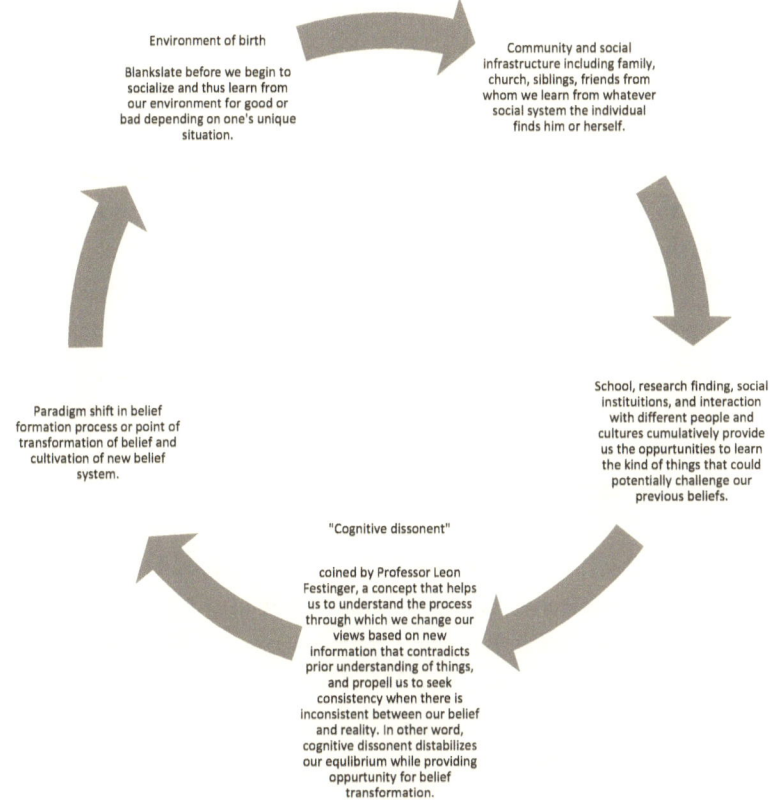

Environment of birth

Blankslate before we begin to socialize and thus learn from our environment for good or bad depending on one's unique situation.

Community and social infrastructure including family, church, siblings, friends from whom we learn from whatever social system the individual finds him or herself.

School, research finding, social instituitions, and interaction with different people and cultures cumulatively provide us the oppurtunities to learn the kind of things that could potentially challenge our previous beliefs.

Paradigm shift in belief formation process or point of transformation of belief and cultivation of new belief system.

"Cognitive dissonent"

coined by Professor Leon Festinger, a concept that helps us to understand the process through which we change our views based on new information that contradicts prior understanding of things, and propell us to seek consistency when there is inconsistent between our belief and reality. In other word, cognitive dissonent distabilizes our equlibrium while providing oppurtunity for belief transformation.

One's observed experiences, materials read regardless of whether they were in the past or present cumulatively, continue to shape one's belief system. This in turn influences how one behaves, as highlighted throughout this chapter concerning the racist behaviors of individuals. In order to understand one's belief system, one must become familiar with the cultural values, biased family backgrounds, and institutions that cumulatively shaped one's belief, as in the case of Derek, Roof, and now James Alex Fields in the Charlottesville case. Each society or individual within the society has culture-specific knowledge of his or her group, and this specific knowledge combines to shape one's belief system. For one to truly understand the behavior of others, the individual must first understand him or herself by genuinely asking and honestly responding to questions such as: What influences human behavior? What informs one's belief system, and how does that lead one to hate to the extent of doing harm to others? One's experience from childhood with siblings, parents, and the entire members of one's community or the company one keeps answers the above questions; we are the company we keep. An individual's relationship with those companies cumulatively factors into one's belief system that is racist as exemplified in the case of Derek as narrated by Ali Saslow's article in the *Washington Post* (Oct. 16, 2016), where the writer quoted Derek's father (Don Black) describing his racist son, Derek Black, as having "All my strengths without any of my weaknesses." Digging deeper, we uncovered the connection that existed between Derek Black's father and mother and their relationship with KKK leaders David Duke. Again, as previously stated when Derek was first introduced in this book—the connection and the impact of the company one keeps intentionally or unintentionally shapes one's behavior (like father, like son).

In his *Washington Post* piece, writer Ali Saslow described Derek as follows: He was not only a leader of racial politics but also a product of them. Derek's father, Don Black, had created Stormfront, the internet's first and largest white nationalist site with 300,000 users and counting. Derek's mother Cleo, associated with one of the country's most infamous racial zealots, David Duke, who became Derek's godfather. They raised Derek at the forefront of the movement and some white nationalists had begun to call him "the heir." It's not surprising that Derek became a racist. His upbringing, the family (father and mother as well as the company he was socially cultured within) cumulatively provides enough for one to draw conclusions as to why Derek turned out to be a racist. It was predictable, and no one should be surprised, considering the kind of people he associated with, a web of racist connections and relationships. Now that we understand the process of belief formation as it relates to Derek's racist belief system, we can now dive into exploring the concept of belief transformation, which we will get to in a moment.

Belief transformation process for Derek.

Obviously, by training and knowing Derek's upbringing, Derek was expected to lead the white nationalist lifestyle, which he did and did it so well – until his transformation of belief occurred in college. As Derek turned 27, instead of leading the movement, he became exposed to new people other than his racist parents and the company they kept. He no longer chose to be immersed in it (racist groups). With new company and new experience, Derek began to untangle himself not only from the national movement but also from a life he no longer understood. From the very beginning, that life had taken place within the insular world of white nationalism, where there was never any doubt about what "whiteness" could mean in the United States. Derek had been taught that America was intended as a place for white Europeans and that everyone else would eventually have to leave. He was told to be suspicious of other races, of the United States government, of tap water, and of pop culture. His parents pulled him out of public school in West Palm Beach at the end of the third grade when they heard his black teacher say the word "ain't." By then, Derek was one of only a few white students in a class of mostly Hispanics and Haitians. His parents decided he would be better off at home, an imperfect environment in which to mold their child into their likenesses, an environment Derek did not create but had no other choice but to live within. Don Black, Derek's father, had grown up in Alabama, where he joined a group called the White Youth Alliance in the 1970s. The group was led by David Duke, a white supremacist leader who, at the time, was married to Derek's mother Chloe. That relationship eventually dissolved, and years later, Don and Chloe reconnected, got married, and together they had Derek in 1989. They moved into Chloe's childhood home in West Palm Beach to raise Derek along with Chloe's two young daughters. Don and Derek always stayed with Don's friends from the white power movement, and soon Derek had heard many of their stories. Stormfront[55] was formed in 1995 and its motto was "White pride worldwide." Over the years, Don's website attracted all kinds of extremists: Skinheads, militia groups, terrorists, and holocaust deniers.

---

[55] "Stormfront - White Nationalist Community". 2019. *Stormfront.Org*. Accessed March 29. https://www.stormfront.org/forum/.

According to the Southern Poverty Law Center, a hate watch group, a handful of the people who posted on Stormfront, had gone on to commit hate crime, including killings. One message board user shot and wounded three children at a Jewish day care center in Los Angeles in 1999. Another killed his Jewish neighbor in 2000 in a town near Pittsburgh. Most likely, Derek had learned from and been influenced by some of these atrocious activities. The good news is that, somehow, external factors such as school changed Derek's life trajectory.

Derek's racist beliefs changed as a result of his exposure to a new environment, devoid of racist family and groups that trained and inspired him to be part of the racist group, and it is interesting to see how it unfolded. After graduating from high school, Derek enrolled in a college in Sarasota. He attended an introductory college meeting about diversity and concluded that the quickest way to be ostracized was to proclaim himself a racist. He decided not to mention white nationalism on the campus and that became the point at which Derek began his journey of transformation, as demonstrated by the transformation of belief diagram below:

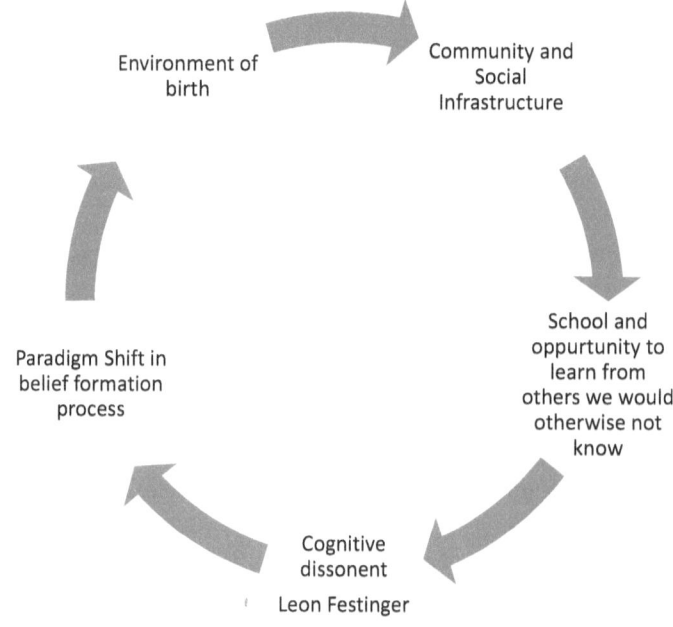

Although Derek was saved by the new company, college made him aware of other people who had no control over their environment, in which their parents and relatives subjected them to hate. These individuals had no opportunity like Derek to transform themselves. The Southern Poverty Law Center cited these people as a hate watch group.[56] These were people who had similar experiences as Derek did. The only difference was that they had no opportunity to transform their belief system as Derek did through school experience and engagement with people who saw the world from a different point of view that transformed him. This is why we believe that these children are victims of the cowardly adults that indoctrinated them into such a life of hate and bigotry. Some people may not agree with us, but there is no question that the so-called white supremacist, nationalists, etc. were groomed in whatever environment they found themselves in. In most cases, they did not have any control over such environments, especially as children. These are people like Dylann Roof, whose life purpose was to start a race war, and now his life has been ruined, and those who contributed to the belief system that nurtured him will never acknowledge what they did. Now the young man is on death row, and others like him go on doing one atrocious act after other. In the most recent incident, a young man named James Alex Fields used his car to plow into a crowd in which he killed Heather Heyer. James Alex Fields' racist behavior again was recognized early in his life by his teacher, Derek Weimer. In an interview with the *Cincinnati Enquirer*, Derek Weimer confirmed that indeed Mr. Fields was a student of his and he went further to describe him as a student to whom he taught history at Randall K. Cooper High School.[57] He remembered James as a very bright kid but very misguided and disillusioned. He stated that when Mr. Fields was a freshman, he wrote a report for another class that was "very much along the party lines of the Neo-Nazi movement." Again, in Mr. Fields' case,

---

[56] Gross, Terry. 2018. How A Rising Star Of White Nationalism Broke Free From The Movement. *NPR.* https://www.npr.org/2018/09/24/651052970/how-a-rising-star-of-white-nationalism-broke-free-from-the-movement

[57] Pitcher, James. 2017. Charlottesville suspect's beliefs were 'along the party lines of the neo-Nazi movement,' ex-teacher says. *Cincinnati Enquirer.* https://www.cincinnati.com/story/news/local/northern-ky/2017/08/13/charlottesville-suspects-beliefs-were-along-party-lines-neo-nazi-movement-ex-teacher-says/563139001/

there were early signs that his experience fits into Mark Twain's assertion that "where you live really does shape who you are."

In conclusion, as a society, we must not only condemn evil deeds, we must provide people the opportunity to engage in transformation and overcoming the violent acts of yesterday while imbuing and encouraging an approach that fosters human-to-human connection. Above all, we must increase efforts to encourage people to use strategic choice as a model while confronting the seeds of violence that are still present, especially in the field of racist behavior, as we recently witnessed in Charlottesville, Va. This chapter without a doubt shows that racist behavior did not and doesn't occur in a vacuum. The people present in these people's upbringing and the accounts from people who knew them before expressed that they had shown signs of extremist views. If these two men had the opportunity to learn from new associations other than the racist people that they were exposed to earlier in life, they could have gone through the belief transformation process and probably would be like Derek, who transformed his belief system. These individuals could have changed into human beings that care for equity and social justice for all. We should encourage more human-to-human engagement and embrace the power such engagement possesses when it comes to changing life trajectories as Derek experienced. Above all, we must embrace Gandhi's enduring words: "Be the change you wish to see in the world."

To foster the opportunity for a change, I would suggest the following:

Race is clearly one of the critical issues of our time. We constantly encounter challenging issues associated with race and racism in our daily lives. It's only through the belief formation process and transformation, as well as being aware of the pain and anguish both perpetrators and particularly the victims are subjected to that we can truthfully and comprehensively answer the big question of where do we go from here to not only eradicate racism and discrimination that stems from it, but also to prevent anyone from going through the same pain and anguish that is often associated with racism?

Answering the above question is extremely important, but I would like to add another question that many in some ways relate to the first question. The additional question then becomes, why is it that despite public concern about race and racism, we still so often hear, see, or read about racist acts, especially to minorities in the form of racial discrimination? And what can be done to eradicate the culture racism and the hate associated with it, and how can we as a nation transform our society and eradicate elements of racial misconduct? The answers to the above questions are vital to addressing racism and racial discriminatory acts.

Earlier, we demonstrated how people change through the belief transformation process, which took us to the concept of cognitive dissonance, a process through which one acquires new information that challenges one's accepted perception, and with the advent of new information, one can employ the new information in order to cultivate a new belief, one that drives change in one's perception over a period.

Now that we have gained a better understanding of belief formation, which drives all sorts of human behaviors, including racist behaviors, which are present in the form of discriminatory practices whether it's overt or covert, the bigger question remains: where do we go from here?

Again, organizations should conduct the situational analysis of the current status of their diversity and inclusion policies and practices in general. More specifically, each organization, as stated previously, should establish an ad hoc committee to study the situation and recommend a plan of action to fight racism and racial discrimination in our society and help others fight racism in all its forms.

We know that racism and racial discrimination are pervasive in our society. They comes in overt as well as in covert forms, and we should do what we must to combat racism and racial discriminatory practices. To address this situation, every organization must begin by designing policies and practices in the organization that will help address the issue of racism and discrimination that causes racism and racial discrimination practices in the workplace.

Furthermore, organizations must include policies that address the issues of race, racism, and racial discrimination in the workplace regardless of whether they are public or private. The policies must unequivocally state: Racism and the discrimination it brings about in the workplace will not be tolerated, and anyone that engages in racist acts, whether overtly or covertly, will be held to account and treated and dealt with accordingly, including counseling, workshops, and even job termination.

Second, there must be a comprehensive strategy to eradicate racism and the resulting discriminatory practices. To ensure the effectiveness of an organization's action to eradicate racism, one must begin by building partnerships with all individuals within the organization. These partnerships should consist of both men and women from all races who will be committed to fighting all types of racist and discriminatory acts, regardless of what forms they take.

Thirdly, all organizations must provide regular training on race and racial discrimination issues. The training must inform workers of the issues and behavior associated with racism, the acts that constitute racial discrimination and other relevant issues in relation to race and racism. The policies and expected practices should be a guide for regular workshops and provide assessment metrics designed to measure improvements that will serve as the basis for further training on issues associated with race and racial discriminatory practices. The envisioned training practices should consistently strive for the improvement of race relations in the work environment that is devoid of discrimination.

The goal of each training or workshop on race and racial discrimination related issues must be clear on the objectives. The desired outcome must be clearly defined and concisely stated. For example, if one is working on a workshop with the purpose of tackling racial discriminatory practices, then that should be clearly and unambiguously stated. Also, race and racist acts must be stated in terms of what constitutes racism or racial discrimination, as well as the expected outcome of the workshop, such as: By the end of each training session, participants will be able to:

Define what constitutes racism or racial discriminatory behaviors and what it means in the context of their work, home, and communities.

Understand the organization's policies, procedures, and efforts necessary to provide equal opportunities to all regardless of one's race.

Clear articulation of acceptable and unacceptable behaviors in the workplace as they may relate to race and racial discrimination.

Develop handouts on what constitutes racism and discrimination, and actions that reflect best practices of dealing with racism and discrimination, and other issues associated with equity and social justice for all.

In conclusion, I believe that the only way to tackle racism and racial discrimination and the violence it contrives is to employ more aggressive and comprehensive policies that address what constitutes racism and discriminatory practices in any organization.

Finally, organizational leadership must commit to continuously train employees on issues related to race and racial discrimination. With an open exchange of ideas, perhaps participants will become more conversant with the issues associated with race and racial discrimination and other equity issues in their complex forms. I believe that with open exchange, participants in conferences and other engagement-driven activities will be encouraged to develop a road map for understanding issues equity and social justices, especially in the area of best practices in the public space.

REFLECTION ON THE CHAPTER

As you finish reading the chapter, please reflect on how it resonates with you in the context of your past, present, and how the future looks. Please consider the past and your present experience as you proceed. As you think through those experiences, be specific as to how the chapter relates to your unique experience Try to connect some of what you read to your own experience or the experience of other people that you know.

_____

_____

_____

_____

_____

_____

_____

If you were able to relate or make connections, based on those connections you made, in what ways would you relay such powerful information to provide learning opportunities to others, especially young people?

_____

_____

_____

_____

_____

_____

_____

In what ways has the content of this chapter helped you to ignite your metacognition while linking those experiences to multitudes of other experiences? As you reflect, please discuss how your experiences help foster meaningful understanding of the issues from one or more perspectives.

_____

_____

_____

_____

_____

_____

If you have no relatable experience, please feel free to express that too. The aim of this chapter is to keep engaging with one another in exploring these issues. We cannot solve these issues by isolating them or pretending that they don't happen.

_____

_____

_____

_____

_____

_____

PART 2

INTERNATIONAL BELIEF SYSTEM

CULTURAL FRAMING IN BELIEF FORMATION: UNDERSTANDING CULTURAL DIFFERENCES IN SHAPING DIFFERENTIAL HUMAN BEHAVIORS

CHAPTER 7

DIFFERENT CULTURAL PERSPECTIVES

There are unimaginable things happening in all parts of the world. Some behaviors are accepted in one culture and despised in others (e.g., child brides, abortion). However, some behaviors are uniformly considered to be extreme and, in the opinion of this author, should not happen anywhere (e.g., caste system, child marriage, which will be both covered momentarily). In general, those behaviors that are extreme are the kind of behaviors that are beyond the threshold of acceptance and thus should be unacceptable in any culture. In other words, these are the behaviors that go beyond the cultural relative theory's driven defense. These behaviors, I believe, should be perceived to be universally wrong in all cultures, even though some are not (e.g., terrorists targeting innocent people, child marriage, and the caste system).

There is a collective cultural agreement that some of those behaviors must be stopped regardless of the geographical location or culture in which it may be acceptable and in fact occurs despite our global cultural agreement that certain acts such as terrorist acts in which innocent people (e.g., children) are targeted and killed still exist. In general, there is a consensus that certain acts should never happen, regardless of cultural locations. Most human beings generally agree that things like terrorist acts, child marriage, and the caste system should not happen in any place in our global community, however, there are acts that still happen and are acceptable in certain cultures, such as child labor. The pressing question is why child marriage should and child labor, even slavery, be condoned and accepted in some cultures under the guise and argument that they should not be excluded from what should be stopped based on a cultural relative argument.

Clearly, these are behaviors that should and must be fought internationally to be eradicated regardless of where it occurs in our global community. These are the kind of behaviors that all people with no exception should agree to and be considered as terrible and need to be stopped. Those who claim that their cultures propel them to engage in those heinous activities should be stopped as well. Besides terrorist acts, there are other activities that some people engage in that should be fought and eradicated completely from the earth, such as racism, discrimination, child marriage, slave labor, mistreatment of women, and even the ideological claim of cultural permissiveness to the victimization of others, such as sexual harassment among others. These are the kind of unacceptable human behaviors that must also be stopped and eliminated completely from the earth.

These behaviors, I feel, should not be tolerated regardless of cultural claims in which the perpetrators may conveniently advance all forms of defense mechanisms aimed at sustaining despicable acts such as racism and all other forms of xenophobia-driven behaviors. Before we go any further exploring the cultural issues that are often cited as the basis for some of these unreasonable claims, let's first explore the concept of belief formation that cultivates the mindset that drives all human behaviors of one's belief system.

One's belief system shapes the individual's perspective and thus propels one to behave the way he or she behaves. As humans, our quest to gain a deeper understanding of belief formation and transformation through a deliberate process and intentional engagement and dialogue with others, especially those whose perspectives are different from ours, opens for acquisition of new knowledge, one that would hopefully result in our learning and gaining a new understanding of how one's belief system is formed. A belief system influences human behavior whether for good or bad.

In the next section, we will explore the power of the belief system, and how the belief system informs human behavior. Subsequently, we will explore the impact of culture in shaping one's perspective, especially those with whom we may disagree. In addition, we will explore how one's belief system could be modified, especially when it contributes to despicable thoughts and behaviors one may have held. In the next section, we will also explore the belief formation process with a focus on cultural relativity and consequently look at the means through which belief systems could be modified or completely transformed through the process of belief transformation.

Belief Formation, Modification, or Complete Belief System Transformation.

As humans, we are social beings and our belief systems are formed by experiences through the company we keep. Paramount in the formation of our belief systems are shared history, ideas, and cultures along with the values shared with loved ones, such as parents, siblings, and friends, among others. The formation of our belief system is not unique to any single culture; it's pretty much the same in all cultures and it is dynamic. We are the company we keep, including the culture in which our belief systems are formed. These are the people who contributed prominently in shaping one's cultural belief system. We normally trust them and they are often the source of our inspiration. The accumulated experiences we gain from those we love to a great extent influence our behavior regardless of cultural differences. This is because they are within the company we trust and respect. Ultimately, they tend to behave in ways that are consistent within the context of culture and behaviors.

Take for instance what happens when an American child is introduced to Santa Claus in a social and cultural environment where the child learns and develops a belief system based on America's cultural interpretation of what Santa Claus means. As far as culture goes, the child's cultural perspective will undoubtedly reflect the child's cultural perspective of Santa Claus.

The child's perspective of Santa will be shaped by experience within the context of America's cultural interpretation of what Santa represents. Clearly, the child's perspective of Santa would cumulatively help shape one's belief system in the context of how the child perceives the meaning of Santa Claus.

As stated earlier, if you were born and grew up Christian in the United States, you would probably have eased into believing in Santa Claus from America's perspective. In that case, you would have perhaps been convinced to believe in the power of Santa Claus and his ability to shower you with great gifts during Christmas. This becomes one's conceptualized belief your loved ones led you to believe, even though their view may or may not necessarily be true. It is what you happen to believe at a point in time in the context of a specific cultural background that shapes the child's belief. A belief system that shapes one's background and the company such person keeps, including the people you trust, believe in, and love does not change easily. As one grows up and learns, he or she realizes that there is no Santa Claus placing Christmas gifts under the tree as led to believe by those you love and trust. This is when you begin to doubt what you have been led to believe about Santa and how you associate Santa's responsibility in scheme of life. However, through questioning and observation, the reality slowly begins to sink in [there is no Santa Claus], and consequently triggers a belief modification or transformation of one's belief system which will be explained further in a moment.

Modification of the belief system or belief transformation

Now that you have realized that the stories that you were told about Santa Claus are not necessarily true, one begins to ask their loved ones' obvious questions about Santa Claus. "Why was I lied to about Santa Claus all these years?" As you pose the above question to square the contradictions between what you had been told and reality, you begin to develop cognitive dissonance, which we examined in Chapters Two and Three. Please refer to those chapters if you need to. When you found out that what you were told about Santa Claus was neither true nor real, as you proceed in your search for the truth, you add new information that sometimes contradicts the previous view. As a result, you strive to balance and be at equilibrium, a perspective that is in sync with what you see with your naked eye, without any more misconception. As a result, you begin to modify your previous belief system or experience what some would characterize as a paradigm shift in your perception of Santa Claus from old to new beliefs through new information via research. With new understanding, you change your view to reflect current research, authentic reality, or new findings as new truths are revealed. The quest to imbue and use new information in our new belief system aligns with John Dewey's view when he stated, "As new discoveries are made, new truths disclosed, and new opinions change with change of circumstances, instructions must change also and keep pace with time" (John Dewey, Freedom and Culture, 1939, p. 157). Clearly, this concept of using new and authentic information should guide our beliefs, and when necessary, change our beliefs or embrace a new paradigm with a new perspective that informs us on new research or new information. As we move forward on other issues, such as child marriage driven culture, the transformation of beliefs that foster the change we seek help reverse those unacceptable behaviors (e.g., racism and all other forms of discrimination) that should be eradicated from the face of the earth. The diagram below illustrates belief formation and how it influences societal behavior such as child marriage and caste system driven society such as found in India.

Diagram on Belief Formation Process

Cultural Impact of Belief Formation that drives cultural behaviors such as child marriage and cast system in Indian

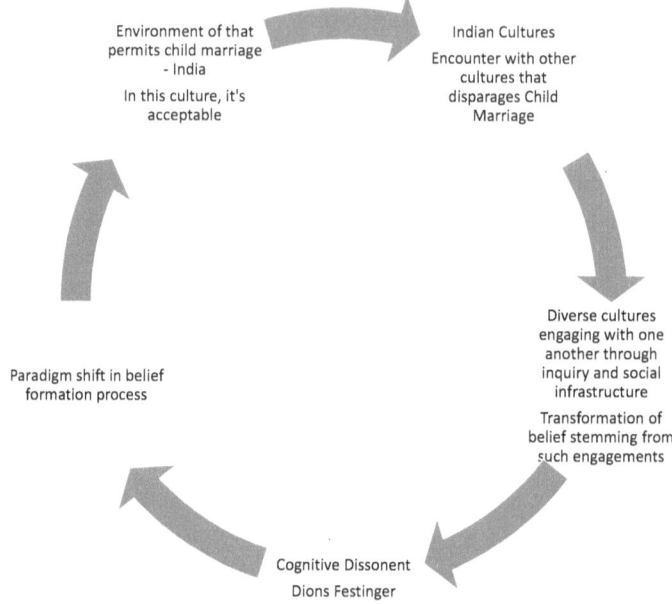

As we have seen from the above diagram, one's cultural belief system is a function of the individual's collective internal and external experiences, which includes, among others, cultures, religion, gender, families, ideation, communities, and the entire company one keeps. Remember the assertions of Twain, Khaldun, and Marx of how humans shape their beliefs. They especially illuminate and explain how our experiences inform our belief system, which thus drives our behaviors, as will be shown in subsequent chapters on child marriage and caste system.

What drives these behaviors?

As we had discussed in the previous chapters, one's cultural belief system is a function of the individual's collective internal and external experiences, experiences that include among others, culture, religion, gender, family, ideation, communities, and the entire company one keeps. Mark Twain's quote helps to explain why people from different cultures tend to live by their different generic cultural norms, values, and experiences that cumulatively influence the formation of each culture and their cultural belief system as we'll see in India's culture of castes and child marriage. For instance, child marriage is illegal and considered a crime in many countries. In the United States, a marital union between an adult to a person under the age of eighteen years cannot take place under any circumstance, the only exception being for sixteen and seventeen-year-olds with parental permission, or those marriages approved by a judge. In contrast, the situation is different in India and other countries whose cultures accept the idea of adults marrying children young enough to be their grandchildren in some circumstances.

The difference in our belief systems stems from our cultural experience, as we will see when one compares how culture shapes the law into the "dos" and "don'ts." For instance, marriage and the Indian caste system are both a common practice and neither is considered to be an offensive act in India as compared to here in the United States, where both child marriage and the caste system would be considered illegal and punishable by law. Neither child marriage nor the caste system is taboo; this is because Indians' collective internal and external experiences shape their view of child marriage and India's caste system is based on their cultural norms. For some, it's normal, and in other places, it may, in fact, be expected.

Ethnocentrism, and the influence of ethnocentrism in human behaviors.

Often, each society believes in the inherent superiority of their own culture with a tendency to view other cultures from their cultural perspective, and in the west, we are notorious for that. In India, where their culture permits child marriage and a caste system, people tend to see those from their cultural perspectives, and that significantly influences perspective of eastern cultures in the west. Let's concentrate on child marriage and the caste system in places where what we consider as wrong and unethical are accepted in their culture and they are using cultural relative theory to defend these acts.

Child marriage

Child marriage could be described as a situation where children are pushed into marriage with people who are significantly older than they are. Some of the perpetrators are old enough to be the victim's grandparents. In fact, child marriage is celebrated in India and other counties that believe in it. The situation surprisingly has a lot in common with our discussion on people's view of Santa Claus. Those who were born and raised in India largely support child marriage. In fact, they are culturally trained and indoctrinated into believing in child marriage and they are taught that there is nothing wrong with child marriages from an Indian cultural perspective. This is the explanation of their cultural perspective.

In order to understand the powerful influence of culture and the company one keeps in fostering human behavior, perhaps one needs to put him or herself in the shoes of those from different cultural experiences, just as we had illustrated with perception of Santa in the eyes of American kids growing up in America. Obviously, hearing and learning from loved ones their view of Santa shapes the individual's view that Santa Claus brings gift during Christmas, especially when one behaves well. Assuming for a moment that you were from a culture that espouses child marriage and perhaps that you were led to believe in one's cultural perspective of child marriage regardless of how repulsive it may be in one culture, it may not be so in another culture. This is especially the case when the information comes from the people you trust. Their view may or may not necessarily be true, but it's just what you happen to believe at that point in time.

Therefore, one acts accordingly at the time. Well, as one grew up and learned, you realized that it's a repulsive and indefensible act that you were led to believe made acceptable by those you loved and trusted.

Despite our understanding of how despicable child marriage is, the practice still continues to take place in various places around the world. There are people who still support this outrageous act.

Alexandra Ma of the *Huffington Post* wrote about child marriage. In her article, she quoted a bystander who witnessed a child marriage. "I was jogging, but my feet froze when I saw her." The bystander saw a young girl in a wedding with a groom old enough to be her grandfather.[58]

There were two responses to the marriage issues; on one hand, there were those who were congratulating the groom, to which the groom responded by simply saying "Thank you." The groom seemed happy and continuously waved to those that supported him and was visibly smiling. The supporters of child marriage would argue that this reflects their cultural and shared values. These are components of their ethnic societies. Even laws permitting child marriage cumulatively helped supporters of this despicable act, which is perceived differently by those supporting and even appeared to be joyful as they expressed their solidarity in support of the groom.

On the other hand, there are those who argue that it's cultural and we should not impose our cultural values on another peoples' culture. Although there are bound to be people who believe in these inappropriate acts, claiming that their culture permits such behaviors, it is heartening to know and realize that the world community is reacting and fighting to eradicate the false premises from which those beliefs are shaped. Similarly, the caste system as it is utilized in India fits and is accepted there, is something that is inconceivable in the United States.

---

[58] Ma, Alexander. 2015. Staged Wedding Shoot Highlights Heartbreaking Reality About Child Brides In Lebanon. Huffpost.Com. https://www.huffpost.com/entry/kafa-video-child-marriage-lebanon_n_5668a13ae4b0f290e521de48

REFLECTION ON THE CHAPTER

As you finish reading the chapter, please reflect on how it resonates with you in the context of your past, present, and how the future looks. Please consider the past and your present experience as you proceed. As you think through those experiences, be specific as to how the chapter relates to your unique experience. Try to connect some of what you read to your own experience or the experience of other people that you know.

_____

_____

_____

_____

_____

_____

_____

If you were able to relate or make connections, based on those connections you made, in what ways would you relay such powerful information to provide learning opportunities to others, especially young people?

_____

_____

_____

_____

_____

_____

_____

In what ways has the content of this chapter helped you to ignite your metacognition while linking those experiences to multitudes of other experiences? As you reflect, please discuss how your experiences help foster meaningful understanding of the issues from one or more perspectives.

_____

_____

_____

_____

_____

_____

If you have no relatable experience, please feel free to express that too. The aim of this chapter is to keep engaging with one another in exploring these issues. We cannot solve these issues by isolating them or pretending that they don't happen.

_____

_____

_____

_____

_____

_____

CHAPTER 8

MUSLIM EXPERIENCES IN THE UNITED STATES

As the wars in the Middle East rage on, little is said to remind people that these warring factions had lived in peace for decades. I am referring to Muslims, Christians, and Jews. They had lived in relative peace prior to the present. For historical reference, Bob Temple (2003), reminds us that "From the 15th century until the end of World War I, the part of the Middle East that includes Syria, Lebanon, Palestine, Jordan, Iraq, and part of northern Africa were ruled by Turkey, which was then called the Ottoman Empire."

People from these areas were known as the Turks, and they immigrated to America just like every other group. They came for new opportunities; some were fleeing religious persecution or running from discrimination to the New World—America. Although people immigrated to the United States for a variety of reasons, most were seeking personal, religious, or economic freedom that was often not available to them in their home countries. The primary reason for immigration, however, was poverty, and to some extent, it remains the case even today. People left their home countries, where they earned low wages and the standard of living was poor, to come to America in an attempt to create a better life for themselves and their families. This remains as one of the main reasons why people are still immigrate to the United States of America as well as other countries.

Historically, immigrants typically moved to the United States as they fled from poverty, wars, lack of freedom, and now there are a host of other additional reasons. In other words, different people are drawn to the United States as well as other parts of the world for a variety of reasons as stated above. With the current global situation and the media influence, different people are now propelled and motivated to come to the United States, as in the case of Mostafa Hassoun immigrating from Syria to America.

Mostafa Hassoun's Experience Coming to America

Mostafa Hassoun's immigration sheds light on various unique and personal circumstances that cumulatively motivate people to come to the United States. It shows the confluence of old and new factors that influence current immigrants' decision to migrate into the United States. In fact, Hassoun's case exemplifies and illustrates old and new factors that cumulatively factor into individuals' decisions, including traditional factors, such as running from poverty, ideological exclusion, and war, as well as the current multimedia influence. In Mostafa's case, one could even argue that he may have been influenced to immigrate to United States for several reasons, including his contemporary connection with an American lady who tutored him in Basic English language. The fact that Mostafa Hassoun learned basic English, as we will see, helped him in his quest to emigrate to America from Syria.

The fact that Mostafa Hassoun learned basic English prior to getting here helped him integrate better into the community, as narrated by Abdo Elkholy in *Arab Moslems in the United States*. His reasons for traveling to the United States were both economic and political. His society at the time was part of the Ottoman Empire and he was burdened by political and economic submission and a sense of social inferiority for not being a member of the ruling class. In this narrative, he was not unique in his reasons for coming to America. His reason, in some ways, was like many others: the pursuit of better opportunity. We have seen the best things and experiences that remind us of what drove us to come to the United States and we have also seen things that make us question why we did come here. These conflicting views about coming to America are shared and they are exemplified by Mostafa Hassoun's story. Mostafa Hassoun was a 23-year-old Syrian refuge, one of the more than four million that fled Syria after the 2011 civil war and one of the 2,550 people who eventually made it to the United States. Mostafa Hassoun's experience is both hopeful and heartbreaking as narrated in a December 26, 2015 *Washington Post* article by Abigail Hauslohner.

Clearly, Mostafa can't escape from the impact of political ideological constructs and perspectives articulated by the two sides of our political parties, the Democrats and the Republicans. Mostafa is now immersed into our society with two political perspectives represented in normal conflicting ideas stemming from the federal and the state perspectives and ideological bent. While the United States government is working on providing Syrian refugees the opportunities to come to America and to establish new lives as part of the country's humanitarian support, the state leadership under the leadership of Republican governor Larry Hogan opposes this idea. He is one of the many Republican governors who wants to halt the idea of establishing and providing for the resettlement of Muslims especially those from Syria and others characterized as Muslim extremists. These conflicting perspectives cultivated by our two parties and their different ideologies create the conflicting, and quite frankly, a different perspective, which would ultimately shape one's perspectives.

On one hand, Mostafa Hassoun, according to Abigail Hauslohner, found himself "in a place where small-town generosity and kindness collide with political tensions of a growing xenophobia; where Hassoun, who arrived in July, 2015 has found a modest home and modest opportunities just blocks from the mansion occupied by Maryland Governor, Larry Hogan (R), one of the many U.S. governors who wants to halt the resettlement of Syrian refugees in the country."[59]

Mostafa Hassoun's reception was both welcoming and fearful, according to Abigail from the *Washington Post*. On the welcoming side, Hassoun was welcomed by Maria and Jonathan Ulbricht, a Severna Park couple whose daughter taught Hassoun basic English over SKYPE while he was in Turkey. They welcomed him into their home. Maria helped him find a job bagging grocery at the local Whole Foods and a place to live with a couple of other young American men his own age who liked basketball and movies. Other benefits included a free morning sandwich offered by his landlord, who owned the food kiosk at the mall. Maria hugged him when he felt isolated and uncertain of how to make life work in a place so completely divergent from where he came from.

As one would imagine, "Mostafa Hassoun had so much in his heart – happiness, sadness – I need to experience it."[60] Like most Syrians, Mostafa Hassoun had never planned to leave his family or his village of apple trees and olive groves for a strange new world of scheduled friendships, pristine shopping malls, and wide interstate highways. He was supposed to go to college in Syria like his sisters had and become an architect. But the war didn't give him that option. So he is here, trying to find his way.

In six months, he has learned to navigate a strange new culture of doctors' appointments, paperwork, and the quintessential American routine of two jobs and never-ending work. He has learned about insurance and that he is required to have it. He has learned that in the minds of many Americans, Islam equals the Islamic state extremist group, and Syria – the country he fled – equals terrorism.

---

[59] Hauslohner, Abigail. 2015. Support and suspicion: The lonely life of a Syrian refugee in Maryland. Washingtonpost.Com. https://www.washingtonpost.com/local/dc-politics/support-and-suspicion-the-lonely-life-of-a-syrian-refugee-in-maryland/2015/12/25/f813cf28-a7ea-11e5-9b92-dea7cd4b1a4d_story.html?utm_term=.df02aabd5a66
[60] Ibid

Hassoun has committed to helping his people. He pointed out that he is prepared to help any new refugees who come to Maryland needing help. "I can help them and guide them on what to do," he said, "because now I know." Hassoun doesn't know much about Governor Larry Hogan, but he knows that Donald Trump, the billionaire who became the President of the United States, thinks most Muslims should be banned from entering the country. He also knows that many Americans agree with these sentiments. This is evident in the overwhelming support President Donald Trump received from voters, especially those within the Republican Party and Independents.

While Hassoun seems to be learning and understanding America and the reason why Americans love the First Amendment, which allows for different political perspectives represented by our two-major political parties, Democrats and Republicans, as evidenced in his experiences along with individuals that support him, as well as those who are against him and even associate him with extremists that played a role in pushing him out from the family and the country he obviously loves.

There are additional experiences, exposure, and certainly new learning that shapes individuals, like Mostafa Hassoun expressed in an account of his experience with a landlord who turned him down for rent after learning that Mostafa is Syrian. Being turned down by the landlord was not a very good experience, but life experiences are a mixture of both good and not so good experiences. Below is an account of Hassoun's good experience with a police officer.

A police officer once stopped Hassoun on the street while he was carrying the Free Syrian Army's flag, a gift, from an American friend, that represents the dream for a free and democratic Syria. He recounts his exchange with the officer. "He asked me about the flag and why I came to the United States," Hassoun recalls. "He said people called him and were afraid that I was a terrorist because of the flag." After looking at the government paper that identifies Hassoun as a refugee and checking his name in a database to verify his identity, the officer did something baffling to Hassoun. He apologized. This incident was a clear demonstration of American policing at its best.

Hassoun compared his extraordinary experience with the police officer as a good demonstration of quality policing in the States. This incident contrasted with his home country because. back home, soldiers from the Assad government would have killed him for displaying a simple flag.

Mostafa had other experiences, including in the checkout line at Whole Foods in which the *Washington Post* writer highlighted that a woman noticed Hassoun's name tag and asked if he were a Muslim. Hassoun, who was raised Muslim but gave up on religion because he felt that prayers could not stop the war, replied to the customer that he was not a Muslim, to which she replied, "Great! Don't be a Muslim, okay?"

After four years in Turkey, including a 15-month screening process of applications and intensive interviews, Hassoun was the only member of his family granted the opportunity to emigrate to the United States. His two sisters, along with one of the sister's family, are in Sweden. A third sister is about to move to Germany with her family. His father remains in Turkey. Hassoun said they are no longer close. In Annapolis, Hassoun has forged new friendships, discovered good American movies, and hopes to restart his education here in the United States of America.

Two weeks earlier, he had gone to the Ulberchts' house to celebrate Thanksgiving. They ate freshly baked pie and sat around the fireplace playing cards. Hassoun didn't mention that he had awoken the previous morning to learn on Facebook that his cousin and age mate Hassan from the same village had been killed.

Clearly, Mostafa Hassoun's experience summarizes what a teacher I met in Washington D.C. summed up as a shortened version of a life journey that everyone must experience as long as one lives. He stated, "Life is full of challenges, and while you face these challenges, always keep in mind that experience and exposure is life itself." This DC resident, who is an African American, further provides the narrative of his life and challenges he had faced this way:

"We are at a time when dog eats dog." For me, it was a new expression, so I explored further to gain a full understanding of what the expression meant. I probed this Washingtonian to explain what he meant by "dog eats dog." He stated, and I paraphrase here, life is not always a bed of roses. You are going to have hardships, hard times, but you must find a way to adjust to get through it. This Washingtonian provided more of his story as I probed. "I was a schoolteacher with a master's degree. Although I believed they never paid me well, I loved my job, especially when I saw my students doing well. Then it was the best. However, I had the job I loved, but it was ruined by an individual who made false statements about me, but, rather than going through the anguish as a black man, I felt it was better I left it alone. Because black people are often never believed, especially when the people who want to destroy you are all white." He said he taught for twenty-seven years and that he worked with poor black, white, Hispanic, and other immigrants. He remains so proud of what he did. The good thing is that now those students still send him gifts and continuously tell him that they are grateful for what he did for them. "They now come back after so many years, bring me gifts of all kinds. Baseball cards, jeans, and a lot of other things. It was the highlight of my life," he said. "I worked hard for those kids at the time. I did not care whether they liked me. I simply did the right things by way of educating them well and I am proud of the work I did."

He continued, "Now I'm disabled. I have all kinds of health issues. I can only use sixty percent of my left side. I still work, but it's never the same. Now I work at the military store as a store stocker with my master's degree. I don't have a connection to that to help me. I live and work in an environment where who you know is more important than what you know. I know a lot, but I don't know anyone who could help me, and provided you don't have such connections in DC, for the most part, you are professionally ruined unless by sheer luck you get something," he asserts.

This Washington resident captures what life is about: "Experience and exposure cumulatively serve as the key to life; just use it well." This message resonates with everyone that encounters the inevitable challenges that come through experience and exposure and it reminds us of Mostafa Hassoun's experience.

The way out and, in fact, the best way is to engage people, especially those who may disagree with you. Engaging with those you disagree with on diversity issues is not only good for an effective and inclusive relationship with them, it could have a ripple effect on any organization that one may be associated with. This will have a positive impact on any organization that intends to improve their bottom line in a diverse and inclusive society. Such discussions and opportunities to build and enrich an individual relatively through meaningful and collaborative connection through the synergy associated with diversity of ideas would trigger new ideas and opportunities to be more effective.

Despite all these great things that draw different people to North America, it's a mixed bag of the good and the ugly, as the Washingtonian reminded us earlier. "Life is full of challenges, and while you face these challenges, always keep in mind that experience and exposure is life itself." Life and life changes as well as change in one's life perspective and continuous changes based on continuous experiences and interaction with people, especially those with whom we may disagree with, is illustrated in the diagram on belief formation and change of belief system below:

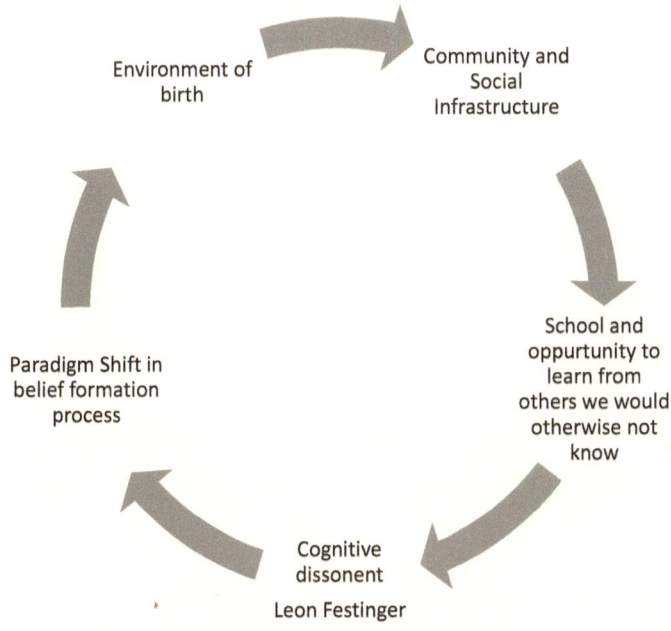

It is fair to say that the purpose of this book is to get people to be thoughtful and to continuously restrain themselves from making snappy judgmental decisions, especially on issues they know little or nothing about. Instead, we encourage and inspire people to focus on meaningful engagement with one another to gain a deeper understanding of various people, their perspectives, and what propels them to do what they do. The content shared is unlike any other; it's a book about self-examination and examination of others, especially those whose perspectives on issues are different from ours.

This book is envisioned as one that would deepen readers' appreciation of themselves and enable people to reflect on their lives and what they do. More importantly, it encourages readers to see others as they see themselves, and thus be apt to put themselves in the shoes of others with the purpose of shaping a more inclusive society, a society that strives for equity and social justice for all. I believe that understanding one another in the context of how an individual's race, gender, culture, social, cultural, sexual orientation, and other environments inform and shape one's belief system and thus drives the individual's behavior is important. To get a good grasp of this book and what it inspires readers to do, one must learn the means to putting him or herself in the shoes of others before making any judgments. By so doing, people will begin to restrain themselves and stop blaming someone before they understand what may have propelled certain behaviors, and instead, to focus on engaging with one another to create a community of trust where people genuinely work collaboratively to foster equity and social justice for all.

REFLECTION ON THE CHAPTER

As you finish reading the chapter, please reflect on how it resonates with you in the context of your past, present, and how the future looks. Please consider the past and your present experience as you proceed. As you think through those experiences, be specific as to how the chapter relates to your unique experience. Try to connect some of what you read to your own experience or the experience of other people that you know.

_____

_____

_____

_____

_____

_____

If you were able to relate or make connections, based on those connections you made, in what ways would you relay such powerful information to provide learning opportunities to others, especially young people?

_____

_____

_____

_____

_____

_____

In what ways has the content of this chapter helped you to ignite your metacognition while linking those experiences to multitudes of other experiences? As you reflect, please discuss how your experiences help foster meaningful understanding of the issues from one or more perspectives.

_____

_____

_____

_____

_____

_____

_____

If you have no relatable experience, please feel free to express that too. The aim of this chapter is to keep engaging with one another in exploring these issues. We cannot solve these issues by isolating them or pretending that they don't happen.

_____

_____

_____

_____

_____

_____

_____

CHAPTER 9

TECHNOLOGY AND THE IMPACT TO HUMAN BEHAVIOR

The speculation about Russians' involvement in our democracy has triggered discussions and debates as to whether technology companies and media organizations ought to be blamed. The case has been made that technology companies at a minimum must do more to combat disinformation and misbehavior such as the one that may have factored into the 2016 American political process – the bedrock of democratic government. There are clearly two perspectives. While on one hand, there are those advocating for technology and media organizations to be held accountable and are asking technology companies to step up and take some responsibility for what people write on their social outlets, and how they use them. On the other hand are the technology media companies such as Facebook, Google, and Twitter, who are by and large rejecting the notion that they should maintain control of what people post on their platforms.

Following what is being speculated as disinformation that drove the 2016 general presidential election in the United States and elsewhere, there has been tremendous discussions in the media and elsewhere as to the authenticity of this election in the United States. The extent to which these allegations are flying with reference to the misinformation in the media has led to the new acceptance by technology and media companies that they should be more responsible for the materials published on their platforms. Many of these technology companies have shifted positions and now agree with those who had criticized them for not having some control over the materials posted on their platform. Now that these technology and media companies are accepting the critique argument and acquiescing and shifting their position to accepting some responsibility, it remains unclear as to what form such envisioned responsibility should be and to what extent it will go.

On the issue of control in the recent congressional hearing, especially in the exchange between Congress and technology representatives, at one point, Former Rep. Trey Gowdy (R-S.C.) quizzed Facebook general counsel Colin Stretch in this way: "Do you think the Constitution protects intentionally false statements?" In response to the question, Facebook general counsel responded, "We are trying to provide a platform for authenticity." Stretch continued, "On Facebook, our job is not to decide whether content is true or false." He explained that the reason Facebook froze Russians accounts distributing divisive political advertisements was not that those ads contained false information, but that the accounts were "inauthentic."[61] In fact, the Facebook general counsel could not have been any clearer as to where he believed his organization's responsibility lay. Obviously, he was not all that concerned about the misleading or outright misinformation that was posted. However, he was obviously very concerned about the authenticity of those postings regardless of whether they were correct or fabricated information.

What is it in our world that cultivates and shapes the attitudes of these technology companies to believe that it is not their responsibility to control what people post on their platform? How did their belief system construct their conception of the notion that they should bear no responsibility for what their creation has fostered – alleged foreign involvement in our political process? To further gain a better understanding of why the technology companies do and defend what they do, one must engage with them in a more meaningful way about what shaped their perspectives,

---

[61] Jurecic, Quinta. 2017. Facebook, Twitter and Google put our ugliness on the market. *Washington Post*. https://www.washingtonpost.com/opinions/facebook-twitter-and-google-put-our-ugliness-on-the-market/2017/11/03/5ffca1ee-c0b9-11e7-959c-fe2b598d8c00_story.html?utm_term=.7b5163389578

perspectives that propelled them to maintain the view that they should not have any control nor bear any responsibility on what those who use their platform post on it.

Again, it comes back to the experiences that shaped their beliefs, and subsequently, their behavior. As we have asserted throughout the previous chapters of this book, our belief system is the core driver of our behavior, and that remains the case regardless of whether it is good or bad behavior. Similarly, technology and media belief systems drive their behaviors, including whether they should be responsible for controlling what people post on their platforms.

To explore the technology companies' general belief systems further, let us spend some time exploring and understanding the technology belief formation process.

Technology and media companies' (Facebook, Google and Twitter) belief formation process

The beliefs of the technology companies are by and large a function of their environment, culture, values, and institutions that shaped them (Organizational Culture), especially their views on the First Amendment of the United States Constitution, which states, "Congress shall make no law respecting an establishment of religion, or prohibiting the free exercise thereof; or abridging the freedom of speech, or of the press; or the right of the people peaceably to assemble, and to petition the Government for a redress of grievances."

Clearly, these technology companies' belief formation process simply reflects their conception of the First Amendment of the United States Constitution. Obviously, the First Amendment influences the shaping of their beliefs as to what their responsibilities are. The technology and media groups' belief systems were informed by their experiences as demonstrated below.

Technology and media belief formation

The diagram below demonstrates the conceptual framework of those in technology, such as Facebook, Google, and Twitter.

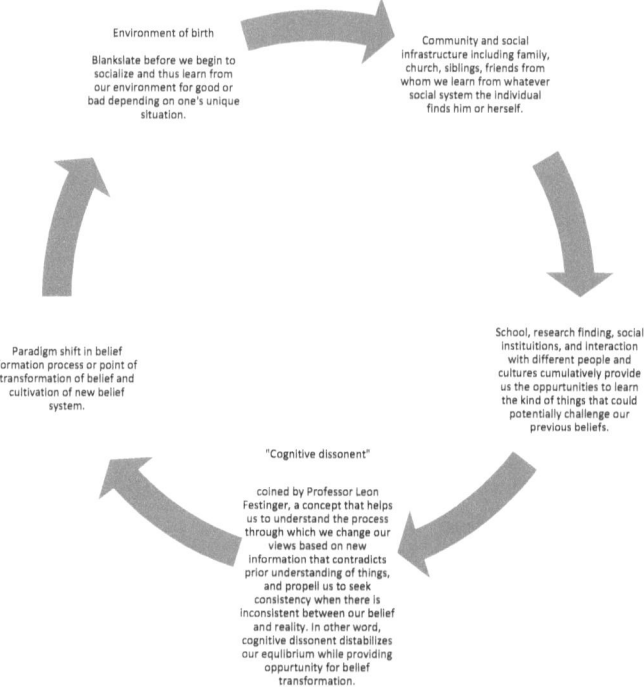

Environment of birth

Blankslate before we begin to socialize and thus learn from our environment for good or bad depending on one's unique situation.

Community and social infrastructure including family, church, siblings, friends from whom we learn from whatever social system the individual finds him or herself.

School, research finding, social instituitions, and interaction with different people and cultures cumulatively provide us the oppurtunities to learn the kind of things that could potentially challenge our previous beliefs.

Paradigm shift in belief formation process or point of transformation of belief and cultivation of new belief system.

"Cognitive dissonent"

coined by Professor Leon Festinger, a concept that helps us to understand the process through which we change our views based on new information that contradicts prior understanding of things, and propell us to seek consistency when there is inconsistent between our belief and reality. In other word, cognitive dissonent distabilizes our equlibrium while providing oppurtunity for belief transformation.

Technology companies such as Facebook, Google, and Twitter are driven by the notion of freedom of expression, and that everyone that posts on their platform should have that freedom to express whatever they choose to express regardless of whether it is disinformation and misbehavior.

Although the pros and cons have taken strong positions to argue their perceptions, both sides remain committed to our democratic process. No one on either side wants a repeat of the disinformation that drove the last general election and that has led to tremendous discussions in the media and elsewhere as to the outcomes of the 2016 election. The allegations are flying with reference to the misinformation in the media and has led to these technological companies accepting that they should be more responsible for the materials published on their platforms. The technology companies have obviously shifted and agreed with those who have criticized them for not having some control with the content and materials posted on their platform.

Technology Companies' (Google, Facebook, and Twitter) Belief Transformation

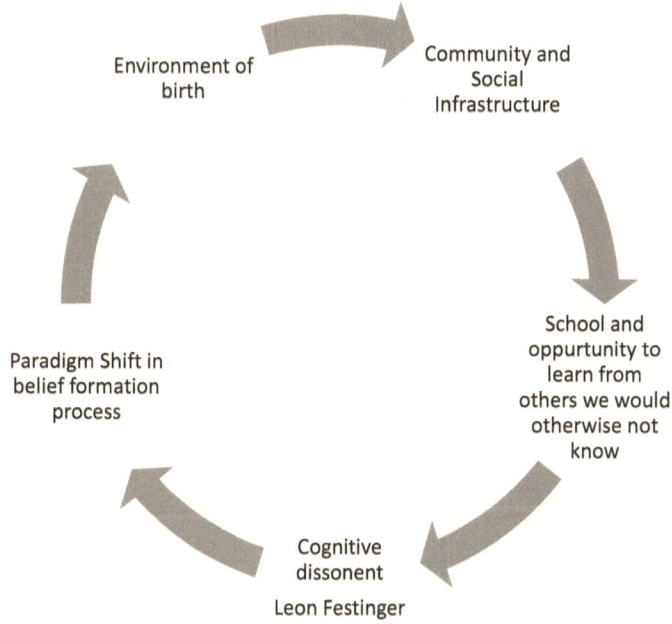

During the exchange, what former Stanford University Professor Leon Festinger characterized as cognitive dissonance, ushered in a new understanding on both sides, which of course demonstrated the process of transformation that would ultimately lead to the middle ground position of understanding, a process through which the new information that propels the companies to change their earlier view to a new and more informed one when it comes to technology companies and the extent of responsibility they must shoulder when it comes to what users post on their platforms. From that conceptual standpoint, the societal role in shaping one's perception as viewed in the shift by the technology organization combining the power of the First Amendment; their observed experiences, materials read regardless of whether they were in the past or present cumulatively shapes the belief system as to what level of control they should have for the public posts.

REFLECTION ON THE CHAPTER

As you finish reading the chapter, please reflect on how it resonates with you in the context of your past, present, and how the future looks. Please consider the past and your present experience as you proceed. As you think through those experiences, be specific as to how the chapter relates to your unique experience. Try to connect some of what you read to your own experience or the experience of other people that you know.

_____

_____

_____

_____

_____

_____

_____

If you were able to relate or make connections, based on those connections you made, in what ways would you relay such powerful information to provide learning opportunities to others, especially young people?

_____

_____

_____

_____

_____

_____

_____

In what ways has the content of this chapter helped you to ignite your metacognition while linking those experiences to multitudes of other experiences? As you reflect, please discuss how your experiences help foster meaningful understanding of the issues from one or more perspectives.

_____

_____

_____

_____

_____

_____

If you have no relatable experience, please feel free to express that too. The aim of this chapter is to keep engaging with one another in exploring these issues. We cannot solve these issues by isolating them or pretending that they don't happen.

_____

_____

_____

_____

_____

_____

PART 3

EDUCATIONAL ISSUES
AND THE NEED FOR BELIEF
TRANSFORMATION

CHAPTER 10

URBAN EDUCATION PROGRAM: A TRANSFORMATIONAL PROGRAM BY A PROFESSIONAL TEACHER ~ MS. MELINDA NWOYE

Every year, I start by building a sense of classroom community among my fourth-grade students. This community fosters a sense of belongingness, security, and respect for others. We are part of a team, and we believe that everything we do should be to better not only ourselves but the lives of others around us. I have often regarded this community of learners as my children. I invest my time and effort into seeing that they succeed. I take time to focus my instructions to meet their mental, social, and emotional needs throughout the school year. The school in which I teach is comprised of a diverse population, including African American, Hispanic Americans, White, Muslim, and Chinese. This school certainly has a diverse team, and every teacher reflects that in both curriculum and teaching practices.

Every good teacher does this too. But is this enough? Not exactly. Why? Because I am not my students. I didn't come from their culture. I am not seen as their race and I don't experience life as they do.

I am white. I was raised Protestant in a rural Pennsylvania community. My school was 99 percent white with one African American family that lived in my neighborhood. I never shared any classes with them. In high school, my physics teacher presented a slide show of pictures he had accumulated throughout his experience in Kenya as part of the Peace Corp. I saw the young children and wanted to go and teach there. At church, missionaries who had traveled to various countries throughout Africa had me determined that I would go there. I wanted to save those children – make a difference. In fact, I never spoke to a person who was not a white Christian until I went to college. The college that I attended was predominantly white as well, so I transitioned easily into my new environment. I didn't know that I was prejudiced. In fact, I prided myself on how I didn't see all African Americans as thieves or dangerous and how I wanted to work as teacher in an inner-city school (after thinking that maybe going away to Kenya would be overwhelming). I saw inner city schools as ones full of children who needed me to come and assist them. I could teach them, and they would be able to break out from the dreaded cycle of poverty and ignorance that plagued their families. Of course, I believed this, I watched others (whites) save inner city African American students in movies. I felt inspired, but something started to change my thinking.

I met my husband, largely in part because I still held out hope that someday I could go save the children in Africa. He was doing research for his doctoral thesis on multicultural education. I knew what that was immediately. He didn't have to tell me because I learned about it in one of my undergrad classes and related it to my experiences in school. Multicultural education involved reading books about other cultures, eating food from other cultures, and even wearing their clothes. Typically, this could be done within a week of school or part of a school night event. In my rural community, this would mostly include learning about different European countries. Italians, French, and Irish were very different, and their foods were always enjoyed by everyone who attended the events. My thinking about multicultural education changed when I was told the true definition. I realized that my education up to that point was mostly Eurocentric. Through my relationship with my now husband, I was introduced to other international graduate students from China, India, and from other countries in Africa. Also, at this point, I was working in the library for an African American woman whom I learned to appreciate and respect. If you would have asked me if I was prejudiced at this point, I would have told you I wasn't because I was friends with people of many different races. And yet, I still had thoughts and attitudes that held me back in my subconscious.

Towards the end of my undergrad program, I had the opportunity to attend the Philadelphia Urban Seminar. It provided rural white education majors the opportunity to work for two weeks in an urban school in Philadelphia. Part of the assignment prior to going was to read the book *Savage Inequalities* by Jonathan Kozol. I cried as I read the part of the book about the conditions of schools in the Bronx and the children who attended them. I was pained because I knew that they deserved a better life. Yet, one part of the book stuck with me and still does to this day. Kozol writes about how every year there is a new fresh crop of teachers that comes to the Bronx to teach. They come to save the children, and within a few years, they are gone. At the time, I was disturbed by the actions of the new teachers because I felt like I would be the one who would stay. I would never leave – *they needed me.* I went to the Urban Seminar, and as I sat in the classroom that was comprised of an African American teacher and African American students, I felt nervous, intimidated, and out of place. I can recall being very intimidated by the classroom teacher. Why? At the time, I had no idea. I had been around other African Americans. I had no idea that my fear stemmed from my thinking that they were so different from me. I didn't know I was scared because I was basing my view of the students and teacher on my deep-rooted stereotypes that still plagued my subconscious. Of course, I was never going to admit that I was racist or prejudiced.

Years later, I was married, now raising three bi-racial girls. I had read many books and articles that included all kinds of advice about how to raise bi-racial children. In one article, the author, a white mom raising her bi-racial (African American and White) daughters, said that she needed to realize that her daughters were going to grow up to be African American women. The old saying, "one drop black" still applied in society. I never thought of them that way, but the words sank in deep to the deepest part of my subconscious, which had been harboring my beliefs about African

Americans. My daughters, whom I loved with every ounce of my being, were viewed in society as African Americans, not as bi-racial. They had brown skin.

Our family moved to Maryland County in the DC metro after living in central Illinois for six years. I moved from an all-white neighborhood to an all-black neighborhood and I was the only white person that lived in my apartment complex or shopped at my grocery store. Often, I joked that people probably thought I got lost. I realized quickly how comfortable I felt. I got to know the check-out cashiers and they recommended places to go out to eat. Of course, I was the only white there too, but it no longer mattered. I started working at a school that was comprised of mostly African Americans, and in the entire elementary school, there were only a few white adults working there. It was difficult for me because I dealt with parents of my students questioning my ability to teach their children. I was white. How could I know how to teach their child? At first, I was very offended. Never in my life had someone questioned my ability to do something based on the color of my skin. I thought, how they could do this to me? But I read Jonathan Kozol's book. I was not giving up. I learned about their children. I learned about what they needed mentally, socially, and emotionally. I appreciated and heard who they were and worked with them to develop the skills and assets to strengthen their position in society. I allowed them to share with me their dreams and supported them as they strived to achieve them. I could hear their voices because I listened. I didn't speak for them. I learned from them. I learned that I didn't need to come and save these kids. Many of the students carried heavy burdens with them to school each day and were stronger than I ever would be. But I also learned that by feeling sorry for a student because of their life circumstances only crippled them and never taught them how to walk on their own. I had always thought that I would sweep in and rescue these children, but they didn't need rescuing. They needed support from someone who would teach them how to carry their load.

I have come a long way in my thinking and realize just how much my early experiences influenced my beliefs. I am consciously aware of my prejudices but don't let them to control my actions. I know that many other people have not had the same experiences as me and it saddens me when I hear through the news presidential candidates making racist and prejudice remarks about groups of people based on their race or religion. I hurt for my students, who are being misunderstood and misrepresented. It is deeply depressing when I hear teachers make statements that are racist or prejudice in nature and yet are unaware of the implications of their words on the lives of those people who they offend. Children are impressionable.

* * *

Throughout this book, we have in one form or another touched on issues of misconception, and how misconception could potentially lead us into wrong decisions, decisions that prejudge our students, teachers, administrators, and other professionals, people we do not know much about. If you have not read Chapters Two and Three, please go back and do so, because Chapter Two provides you with critical information on belief formation that drives human behavior, while Chapter Three demonstrates how certain beliefs need to be transformed to meet our diverse needs. We cannot understand the issues that bedevil us in our schools and workplaces, especially those that stem from our separate cultures, until we become familiar with one another and collectively gain a new understanding of the underlying issues.

Colin Woodard, in his book *American Nations,* highlights the divisions in our society this way: "After the revolution, four of the American nations hurdled the Appalachian and began spreading west across the Ohio and Mississippi valleys. There was very little mixing in their settlement streams, as politics, religion, ethnic prejudice, geography, and agricultural practices kept colonists almost entirely apart in four district tiers." (p173). Woodard continues, "Their respective cultural imprints can be seen to this date on maps created by linguists to trace American dialects, by anthropologists codifying material culture, and by political scientists tracing voting behaviors from the early nineteenth century straight through to the early twenty-first."

Mr. Woodard was correct; however, he missed connecting the dots with reference to separate cultures with the unconscious separation of different minority groups in our schools and workplaces. Mr. Woodard was writing and making important points on the origin of our separate cultures and how it contributes and fosters systemic inequity, whether it's in terms of race or economics, the fact that African Americans are in a place of disadvantage on both fronts, which can be attributed to the historical and current discriminatory practices they continuously endure in our schools and in workplaces.

Unfortunately, the perpetrators of inequity often never have the opportunity to see how their decisions and judgment in educational issues lead to an imperfect outcome when it comes to education of minority students as one of my associates did. My associate's experience quite frankly prepared her well to teach any child and in any place. I assert that she can because she gained the experience that only a few could get, as she pointed out in her own work, "I am consciously aware of my prejudices but don't let them control my actions. I know that many other people have not had the same experiences as me and it saddens me when I hear on the news presidential candidates making racist and prejudice remarks about groups of people based on their race or religion. I hurt for my students who are being misunderstood and misrepresented. It is deeply depressing when I hear teachers make statements that are racist or prejudiced in nature and yet, they are unaware of the implications of their words on the lives of those people whom they offend."

Talking about offending, more importantly, we must go beyond that. Instead, let's talk about how the victims of that offensive language try to navigate, and that brings us to William Gladden Foundation's report. According to the William Gladden Foundation report, "The Effects of Racism and Prejudice on Children" overburdens minority children, and as result, they resort to doing certain things for survival, including:

"Children who are victims of racism and prejudice may react in any one of the following ways:

1. accept the stereotype and develop a sense of inferiority,
2. act out the stereotype,
3. reject his or her ethnic inferiority, or
4. develop hatred or resentment toward the perpetrator." (p 7, 2005)

The William Gladden Foundation report serves as good segue to a couple of articles. The first addresses and provides teachers and administrators a road map to working more effectively with diverse students, and the second article provides parents a step-by-step approach to meeting their students' academic needs, especially for the parents of minority children. Here are two relevant articles.

Academic Achievement Gap: Necessary and Simple Actions to Eradicate it.

For a number of years now, I have worked in the area of education with a focus on curriculum and instructional development. Within this long period, I have learned interesting things about education and the never-ending debates it generates. Furthermore, educators who are trained in curriculum and instruction should be aware of the crucial need to align the scope and sequence of content and instruction to the needs of students. This is essential if we truly want to eradicate the achievement gap. It's so ridiculous that sometimes I wonder why the issues that matter are oftentimes not even included in the debate or discussions amongst the talking heads. It's not that we do not know the real issues but choose to dance around them. Research is clear about inequity in our system and the impact to the poor, especially minorities and African America children, in particular.

James Coleman, an American sociologist, theorist, and empirical researcher, and former president of the American Sociological Association, provided abundant information as to what is ailing our educational system, especially for the children of the poor and minorities. He provided us with the window through which we can understand sociology of education and public policy. Coleman was one of the first to use the term "social capital." His work in Social Theory influenced sociological theory and his life work was epitomized in the "Coleman Report." This report reflects what we are experiencing today as to the inequity of educational opportunity. In 1983, President Ronald Reagan's department of education, led by Terrel Bell, published a report on the state of education. In that report, he reminded us that if a foreign power does to us what we do to ourselves, it would be considered as an act of war, and that is serious. Fast forward, between 1981 to date, and in between, there has been numerous research done, including those done by presidents and others, including Jonathan Kozol, stressing the impact of inequality in terms of opportunity and access, especially when it comes to the educational preparation of the poor and minorities.

The obvious reasons why some students don't perform as their counterparts based on the issues associated with what former University of California Professor John Ogbu characterized as "cultural capital" (privileges in educational funding, child's zip code, parental education, and socioeconomics), among others. Instead of focusing on those critical issues of equity, opportunity, and access, we have focused on irrelevant and ridiculous ones that end up negating research and what we know about teaching and learning. Research provided by American scholars, if implemented, will completely eradicate the educational gap as we know it. We know a lot about teaching and learning, theories of teaching and learning, especially with modern research in cognitive psychology. According to cognitive science, meeting learners in their locations in the learning continuum is critical to fostering meaningful learning; and yet, what do we do? We lump students who are proficient in the subject matter with those who perhaps are three grade levels below and at the same level. It's like putting a student in an advanced calculus with someone who has not done his or her elementary function, so of course there will be gap. In such a situation, you see, the instructor negates the theory of cognition that stresses the importance of meeting a learner in his or her location in the learning continuum. It's a no brainer that there is a gap from the beginning, a gap that will inevitably increase unless we adhere to cognitive theory's position, meeting the learner in his or her location, figure out what the existing gaps are, and helping to bridge those gaps. Unfortunately, that is not what some do in practice. Instead, we engage in discussions framed in terms of "an academic gap between white and black," rather than asking the right question, such as what factors contribute to and drive these persistent gaps. How do we eliminate them and subsequently eradicate the existing academic gap?

In fact, our research professionals have labored to provide us with state-of-the-art guides to help schools eradicate academic gaps. Unfortunately, we have employed all kinds of phrases such as "No Child Left Behind," among others. If teachers are encouraged to spend some time meeting learners at their varied locations in the learning continuum and helping them engage in meaningful rather than meaningless and fragmented information-based exams, the academic gap will be eliminated. If you are asking what the proof is, here is your answer. Take a look at the countries that are outperforming us, such as Finland, Japan, Korea, etc., and ask why are they outperforming us? You will consistently find that they address the issues. That has been the major reason and it continues to impede our nation's ability to prepare all her children. Reasons include poverty, lack of opportunity, and access, among others. For instance, our researchers have done and continue to do phenomenal jobs. They have consistently pointed at some of the basic drivers for meaningful learning, and yet, as a society, we negate those, especially when it comes to preparing the children of the poor or minorities. This is a situation that is often further complicated by unconscious bias of some professionals that is so ubiquitous in our society.

The critical role of teachers to meet learners at their entry points in the learning continuum must be encouraged. Equity and social justice or lack thereof for all has a differential impact on people, depending on the side one finds him or herself. Oftentimes, I hear or read discussions on issues associated with the academic gap. Each time such a discussion goes on, I cringe and feel as though they are re-victimizing the victims of our system. I consistently remind people that research on why we have this academic gap is clear, and perhaps we will continue to have it, unless we confront the root cause of the gap. We can pretty much predict with almost certainty what will happen to a child who does not get what he or she needs to learn, and the implications as to whether or not the person will live a successful life. Research is clear on the academic gap. The problem is the fact that the issues are often swept under the carpet while people, especially those who are uninformed about the issues, continue to engage in talking, which leads to a predictable result – dead end solutions that are driven by images to show off rather than tackling the true cause of academic gap while many assume it's a white or black issue. I am not here to completely dismiss the proposition that it is a black or white issue; I am sure that it contributes in some situations, but the focus here is on the real issue that fosters existing academic gaps in our society.

For starters, there are certainly obvious reasons for anything that happens in life and there are specialists who can pinpoint the reasons and even when it started and forces that nurtured the situation. Well, an academic gap is no different. We could pinpoint the root cause of academic gap and why it continues and perhaps will never go away unless the real issues are confronted. We constantly point to the obvious reasons for academic gaps, which include poverty, school funding, and more importantly, teachers' attitudes (some teachers are formally or informally trained during their formative years to perceive certain students as "at risk." These are students who fall into the category of less likely to succeed. With this kind of mindset, such teachers treat children differently, and these children never gain what they need, such as reading competency or solving problems that are foundational for their future academic success. These are issues that contribute in the creation of an academic gap stemming from whether one's location in the academic continuum promotes or inhibits progress.

Clearly, the children of the poor and minorities are more often victims of our systemic inequality that begins so early in their lives. For instance, the children of the poor, especially minorities, particularly African Americans, are disproportionately disciplined and often suspended in elementary school, as it has been ubiquitously documented in research, for example, by Claudia Rowe, *Seattle Times,* among others. In her piece titled "Race dramatically skews discipline, even in elementary school: The racial gap starts at a young age of 5, and it's persistent," she asserts that when you suspend a child, it's no brainer that the child will be missing classes and opportunities to learn. Furthermore, we must keep in mind that those who are often suspended have a significant gap to start with, so, when you suspend them, you dramatically accelerate the gap, and it continues until the child either gets frustrated and quits or stay frustrated with little or no desire whatsoever to be succeed in what a victim would undoubtedly consider to be a hostile environment. In spite of these experiences the victim may go through, all hope may not be lost if we concentrate on issues that could lead to a shift, the kind that produces positive results.

As I indicated above and elsewhere, the most important determinant of a child's academic success is the teachers' attitude toward the students. The former chairman of Microsoft, Bill Gates, reminds us in his blog, titled "Out of My Shell: A Teacher Who Changed My Life."[62] In that piece, Bill Gates gave credit when he wrote passionately about the people that made a difference in his life. "Three very strong women—my mother, my maternal grandmother, and Melinda—deserve big credit (or blame, I suppose) for helping me become the man I am today. However, Blanche Caffiere, a very kindly librarian and teacher I've never written about publicly before, also had a huge influence on me." Bill Gate reminds the world how he feels about the woman who helped him. "Before she passed, I had an opportunity to thank her for the important role she played in my life, stoking my passion for learning at a time when I easily could have gotten turned off by school."

Well, when we speak about achievement gap, rather than talking heads, why don't we focus on the root cause of it? If we as a society are serious about tackling this issue, why can't we begin by asking critical and right questions, and using stories like those of Bill Gates to contrast those on the other side of our systemic inequity and prejudice? A lot of people love to talk about the achievement gap, but are not fully prepared to do what is necessary to eradicate it. I'm talking about training or retraining teachers, especially those who by no fault of theirs were provided with biased mindsets about the children of the poor and minority, a mindset that they could not divorce from their actual practice.

---

[62] Gates, Bill. 2016. "A Teacher Who Changed My Life". *Gatesnotes.Com*. https://www.gatesnotes.com/Education/A-Teacher-Who-Changed-My-Life

Perhaps we could change this situation by confronting the reality of our biased system. We can begin by accepting the fact that poor and minority students are intentionally or inadvertently treated unfairly when compared with their white or privileged counterparts. We often don't give these victims appropriate credit for being aware of what is happening around them. They see prejudice and know how it feels and yet they go through the system that oftentimes act as if the victim is unaware of what the system does to them. The children of the poor and minorities are overtly or covertly marginalized in some aspects of our society, including in their schools when they are young, in their jobs through employment discriminatory practices they endure, in their search for mortgage loans when they start looking for lenders, and of course, how they are mistreated in our criminal justice system as explained in Michelle Alexander's book, *The New Jim Crow*. They play no role in the creation of poverty in their environment and schools that are ill-equipped to care adequately for their needs based on their location in the learning continuum. They often don't have the privileges the children of rich and famous automatically have and take for granted in our society. Then, oftentimes, these children of the poor and minority come to school with a burning desire to learn, and some get what they need and thus do fairly well. However, some are exposed to teachers whose belief system is biased. Such teachers believe that certain people can't do well regardless of what they do to help, and that for the most part, put the last nail in the coffin of the victim's ability and opportunity to succeed. This kind of treatment creates self-doubt in the victims' minds and ultimately limits the extent to which most victimized students can go in pursuit of their academic and life's goals. I cringe because certain segments of our population are consistently sabotaged and, for the most part, are overtly or covertly limited from achieving their God-given potential.

Imagine these children of the poor and minority, especially African American children, having a teacher like Bill Gates had. A teacher who creates the kind of image imbued in Bill Gates in his 4th grade, especially those that came from the librarian Mr. Gates described as his "maternal grandmother."

As I stated from the beginning, we can eradicate academic gap if we commit to doing what needs to be done. It's not just one single thing that we can do, but we could do a host of other things, including providing training on conscious or unconscious biased mindset that is developed as result of lack of mixing and understanding one another. Such trainings would foster equity and above all demonstrate the role teachers' attitudes play in shaping the academic trajectory of those they touch as exemplified by the teacher and librarian. Bill Gates captures his relationship with his teacher and librarian well when he stated as follows:

> When I first met Mrs. Caffiere, she was the elegant and engaging school librarian at Seattle's View Ridge Elementary, and I was a timid fourth grader. I was desperately trying to go unnoticed, because I had some big deficits, like atrocious handwriting (experts now call it dysgraphia) and a comically messy desk. And I was trying to hide the fact that I liked to read—something that was cool for girls but not for boys. Mrs. Caffiere took me under her wing and helped make it okay for me to be a messy, nerdy boy who was reading lots of books. She pulled me out of my shell by sharing her love of books. She started by asking questions like, "What do you like to read?" and "What are you interested in?" Then she found me a lot of books—ones that were more complex and challenging than the Tom Swift Jr. science fiction books I was reading at the time. For example, she gave me great biographies she had read. Once I'd read them, she would make the time to discuss them with me. "Did you like it?" she would ask. "Why? What did you learn?" She genuinely listened to what I had to say. Through those book conversations in the library and in the classroom, we became good friends.

I believe that anyone who gets the kind of caring teacher as Bill Gates had in his formative years, whether the person is black or white, will be guaranteed academic success and would certainly make the debate on the achievement gap unnecessary. I do believe that there should be no more debate when it comes to issues associated with achievement gaps. We know that the achievement gap exists, and that it does not exist in a vacuum. Rather, it's the experience we put children in their formative years that propels them to strive for the best or create self-doubt that ultimately leads them to poor academic performance. I would even argue that it's not about white or black, it's about the differential quality of education and resources we provide, and above all, it's the teachers' attitude that prominently factor into the creation of academic achievement gaps. If we want to eradicate these gaps, we must change teachers' attitude, and shift it to mirror Bill Gate's teacher and librarian's attitude towards him. If we take that playbook, I am confident that we will eradicate the term "achievement gap" in all its forms. To that end, I would urge anyone who wants to eradicate the achievement gap to first call it what it is. It's about the quality of education we provide to children, and above all, it is about teachers' attitude. It can be achieved when we are able to confront the misconceptions some teachers may have developed in their formative years and rather resort to treating their learners as Bill Gates' teacher, Mrs. Caffiere, did for him.

A Guide to Parents on strategies to bridge the gap and position their children for academic success

Why do we consistently have achievement gaps in our school system? The variation of the academic success between the mainstream and urban and rural poor is real, and it does not occur in a vacuum. We know why there are variations in our children's academic achievement, and we know what could be done to change that equation. It's about changing mindsets. It's about rectifying uneven provision of resources and providing appropriate preparation. It's about eradication of social promotion. It's about leveling the playing field, and yes, it's about breaking the existing artificial walls that divide people and foster the cultivation of conscious and unconscious bias-driven behaviors in schools. If we could openly, holistically, and systematically confront these issues, there would be no doubt that we could overcome the challenge posed by achievement gaps. Unfortunately, although research provides professionals the information that could guide them to overcome these challenges, the information is often discounted through political expedience while the cycle continues.

The problem is not that we do not know how to interrupt this unfortunate cycle; we do know. The problem is that instead of confronting the issues head on, we are sabotaged by those who continuously resort to non-issues, especially by those whose children are not faced with the prospect of low achievement gap. Instead, they resort to changing the subject to some trivial issues. They rather want a different discussion like blame games and other concocted trivial debates that they know will not get to the root of the issues associated with ubiquitous achievement gaps in our system, some act in support of choice as if that would solve all educational problems. Those who advocate for choice as a solution know so well that there is nothing like choice in the truest sense of it. In a free market system, where demand and supply, along with profit and affordability, cumulatively drives everything, they should know better. Does anyone really believe that the poor and the rich will have equal chance for what some characterize as "choice?" Anyone that believes so would need to familiarize themselves with the economic theories of demand and supply and profit-driven decisions in a free market system such as ours.

In a market- and profit-driven society, choice does not really mean choice, otherwise, everyone would send his or her children to Harvard or Stanford. In a capitalist market-driven environment, limited resources for the most part dictate the choice one makes; unless you have the resources in such a market-driven system, there is nothing like choice. In addition to other factors, such as human frailties, it's difficult, especially for those with limited resources. It is a system where the fact that one likes a private jet as a choice for transportation does not mean that he or she can get it; education as choice takes a similar route. That you have choice does not mean you can go to any school you want. There are conditions that don't allow everyone to realize the choice of a private education. The excuses that some people repeatedly give as to the cause of the achievement gap has eaten into the fabric of our society so that it has become normalized, while the real issues are rarely addressed.

Mounting research evidence consistently points to the factors that foster academic success or failure. Those factors were pointed out in James Colman's 1968 report; in 1983, President Reagan's secretary of education, Terrel Bell, as previously mentioned, provided similar information, and went further to warn that if a foreign nation does what seems to be destroying the life trajectories of urban and rural poor, and to some extent, poor white children in rural areas, we would consider it as an act of war.[63] Clearly, the factors that drive academic success or lack thereof had been established and it has not changed much. Fast forward to the litany of reports that persist even as I write this piece, in 2019, and we are still reporting about adults acting as if the children have been provided with what they need to succeed in their high school as well as in college (look at recent DC). It does stop there. Further, read reports of disproportionate discipline and suspension of minority children in some schools.[64]

There are students who are behind from day one due to lack of adequate preparation in reading and other areas. As if they are not behind enough, the system compounds the problem by suspending them, as if the children learn anything during suspension. These are places or communities devastated by neglect, poverty, and culturally irresponsible practitioners.

For parents with young children who are wondering what to do to ensure that their children acquire the competencies necessary to bridge the gap for today and in their future academic endeavors. For people whose experience of education has been negative, especially in urban and rural areas, no worries, help is on the way. In this piece, regardless of your situation, I know the fear is real, the fear that your beloved one, your child or relatives or people you know, are simply not going to get what they need to be successful in school, and by extension, in life. This is especially true when one factors the level of fierce competition that is sweeping our global village. If you are concerned, please pay close attention to the remaining part of this piece. I will provide you with a couple of simple steps you can take to mitigate the situation for your child today and in the future.

---

[63] Kent, James K. "The Coleman report: opening Pandora's box." *The Phi Delta Kappan* 49, no. 5 (1968): 242-245.

[64] http://tinyurl.com/qh4pks6

First, before school begins, make appointment to meet with your child's school officials. It could be your child's teacher, librarian, and other educational resource personnel, including the school principal and other people in the system that could sing the same song you want to sing to your beloved child.

Second, once you schedule for the meeting, do your homework and present the school official or officials with specific actionable activities you would want to engage with them for the sake of your child's education. Please, don't be afraid. Ensure that the school representative is made aware that you know why it's predictable for some students to succeed while others fail. Make it clear that you are concerned and that your concern propels you to meet them to figure how you could help them to help your child along with other children. A piece of advice as you meet the school officials, ensure that you endeavor to treat the school officials with respect, and never speak to any of them in condescending manner, and reassure them that you would be prepared to work with them and do what it takes to ensure that your child succeeds. They would love and will be willing to work with you, and I can assure you that they will if you approach them appropriately.

Share your thoughts with them. Let them know that you want to work with them to ensure that your beloved one's foundation results in meaningful learning and subsequently academic success. Begin by telling them that you understand how difficult it is to teach and encourage students who are discouraged and frustrated in part because they don't know what success is like. It is complicated and let them know that you are aware of all these things, including those students who do not have supportive parents or communities that are there to support them. In addition, quickly reassure the school officials that your beloved one's educational success is a priority for you, and as such, that you are prepared to work with each and every one of the school officials to help and support them in whatever way you can. Tell them that you met a scholar who shared with you what it takes to ensure success for all children, and that the scholar emphasized asking the school officials in what ways they would like you to help.

Then proceed swiftly to suggest what you conceptualized clearly defined steps to foster meaningful learning for your child. Ask the teacher to consider certain steps as he or she works with your child. Tell the teacher that your child may be behind in his or her preparation, and then suggest that you would like certain actions to be taken to ensure that you uncover her weak areas and then work to overcome them so that the problem will be eliminated, and thus prevented from being a problem in the future, then be clear in sharing a step by step approach as enumerated below:

First begin by giving tests to ascertain what the learners already know.

1. In the process, address any misconceptions you may have identified in the course of administering the tests.
2. Start from students' current knowledge level and help them to relate their prior knowledge to new information in meaningful ways.
3. Armed with the information, which is powerful, begin to provide compelling reasons for curriculum and pedagogical adaptation, planning scope and sequencing of learning materials, while imbuing assessment mechanisms to support improvement in all areas of your child's academic and social development.
4. Develop a strategy that fosters two-way communication between the school and the home culture and continuously work with your child's teacher or librarian to ensure that active and meaningful learning occurs and that the activities you both embrace would help bridge the structured and unstructured gaps that could potentially impede your child's learning,

Perhaps if you follow through and work with the school where your beloved one goes, you will prevent him or her from becoming another victim of school's systemic failure in the quality of education the system provides to some of our most vulnerable children, especially the poor in both urban and rural schools.

I close by urging parents to be persistent to ensure that success comes their way and for their beloved one. You know that research is the key for progress in all we do in life, especially in education. I therefore want you to always remember an American educational psychologist and a scholar who reminds us about the power and essence of research in whatever we do this way:

> "As new discoveries are made, new truths disclosed, and manners and opinions change with the change of circumstances, institutions must change also and keep pace with the time" (Dewey, 1939, p.157)[65]

Do not be afraid to revisit John Dewey's statement in 1939, it's as good as it was in 1939, if not better, in our today's competitive global village.

---

[65] John Dewey. (1939). Freedom and Culture, 1939, p. 157).

REFLECTION ON THE CHAPTER

As you finish reading the chapter, please reflect on how it resonates with you in the context of your past, present, and how the future looks. Please consider the past and your present experience as you proceed. As you think through those experiences, be specific as to how the chapter relates to your unique experience. Try to connect some of what you read to your own experience or the experience of other people that you know.

_____

_____

_____

_____

_____

_____

_____

If you were able to relate or make connections, based on those connections you made, in what ways would you relay such powerful information to provide learning opportunities to others, especially young people?

_____

_____

_____

_____

_____

_____

_____

In what ways has the content of this chapter helped you to ignite your metacognition while linking those experiences to multitudes of other experiences? As you reflect, please discuss how your experiences help foster meaningful understanding of the issues from one or more perspectives.

_____

_____

_____

_____

_____

_____

If you have no relatable experience, please feel free to express that too. The aim of this chapter is to keep engaging with one another in exploring these issues. We cannot solve these issues by isolating them or pretending that they don't happen.

_____

_____

_____

_____

_____

_____

CHAPTER 11

URBAN PROGRAM THAT EXPOSED RURAL COLLEGE STUDENT TEACHERS TO URBAN CULTURE

The Urban Seminar is a program I designed and developed to bridge the cultural divide between rural and suburban teacher preparation programs and urban students. This was a program that was operationalized in Philadelphia and Peoria. The focus was to foster human-to-human engagement and understanding among various diverse groups, teachers and students alike. In a piece I did years ago, I quoted Pallas et al, 1989, asserting that by the year 2020, minorities will comprise 48 percent of the nation's children from five to seventeen years of age, and yet only 5 percent of the school teachers are expected to be members of the under-represented groups.[66] Geneva Gay echoed similar sentiment as she pointed out that while public school children are becoming more ethnically racial and linguistically diverse, prospective teachers continue to be predominantly middle class European Americans, a phenomenon that is nationwide. James Banks (1994) argued that even if those with the responsibility of preparing teachers are successfully increasing the percentage of minority teachers by

---

[66] Pallas, Aaron M., Gary Natriello, and Edward L. McDill. "The changing nature of the disadvantaged population current dimensions and future trends." *Educational researcher* 18, no. 5 (1989): 16-22.

85 percent, there will still be predominantly white teachers working with students who differ from them culturally, linguistically, racially, and with regard to social class status.[67] I asserted then, "It is therefore critical that those in the business of preparing teachers do whatever they can to increase the number of minorities in teaching profession."

In spite of all these predictions that are unfortunately for the most part turning out to be correct, the fact is that nothing has been substantially done based on the recommendations made sixteen years ago with reference to increasing minority teachers. Fast forward to today, and let's pose a different question. "Why do we need minority teachers?"

To the above question, based on research then and now, the educational system has repeatedly failed minorities. As I stated in 1999, in an article titled "Urban Seminar," in an effort to make the case for better teacher preparation, I proposed in support of state mandates, school districts and certifying agencies, such as NCATE, to continue pressing and perhaps requiring teacher education institutions to imbue urban multicultural experiences in their teacher preparation program.[68] Clearly, all these issues stem from the continuous deteriorating academic performance of minorities. The problem we face with minority students' academic performance did not seem out of a vacuum; it stems from historical partitioning of people based on their group, and subsequently, leading to marginalization and discrimination of people based on grouping and other cultural differences.

This difference stems from what Woodward (2011) described in his book as historical separation and lack of mixing of different groups.[69] As a result of the lack of mixing, each group develops a mindset that is consistent with belief formation process (which I have addressed throughout the book,

---

[67] Banks, James A. "Transforming the mainstream curriculum." *Educational leadership* 51 (1994): 4-4.

[68] Nwoye, J. & Suzanne Rose (1999) The Value of Urban Seminar in Rural Teacher Training Program in the Journal of Philosophy and History of Education, Volume 49 http://www.journalofphilosophyandhistoryofeducation.com/jophe49.pdf

[69] Woodard, Colin. (2011). American Nations: A History of the Eleven Rival Regional Cultures of North America Kindle Edition

with more emphasis in a moment) that ultimately creates a "we versus them" mentality, which by extension leads to division in schools and jobs that continuously serve as the driver for the inequity we experience today.

In the previous years, progressives have advanced various strategies to address the issues of equity and social justice. Despite these efforts, we have not gotten the desired result. We must admit that while we have made some progress, but not significant enough, there is so much inequity in our society. It comes in different forms, including among others, inequity in schools, jobs, promotions, etc., all driven by the lack of mixing and misunderstanding one another that leads to the creation of the "we versus them" mentality in all aspects of our lives.

This situation of "we versus them" is not limited to teachers; it is the same with the students they teach. In other words, both teachers and students they teach come from different cultures and groups with little understanding of each other, as a result, they developed different mindsets and misconceptions of one another. As a result, teachers from rural and suburban communities are not informed about children in urban schools, and if at all, they are based on misconceptions that are not consistent with the real life of urban children or their communities.

In order to gain a better understanding of one another, we set out in the program to explore how these misconceptions were formed, and more importantly, to understand the impact of one's belief system and how it cultivates and drives these misconceptions and ultimately modify their belief system to reflect the reality of urban children through an urban program and thus better prepare teachers on culturally responsive practices that enable professionals to teach both urban and suburban students as they should and must.

To that end, I would propose a new approach that fosters the new social acculturation of different people to get to know one another and ultimately bridge the existing artificial walls that demarcate people in groups, as Woodward pointed out, and prevents them from meaningful mixing and thus creating a "we versus them" that continuously foster divisions, which leads to discrimination and marginalization amongst groups.

Because of this, our desire to imbue culturally responsive teachers at Edinboro University of Pennsylvania, Indiana University of Pennsylvania, Lock Haven University, University of Wisconsin, and other notable research and progressive institutions across the United States and Britain, are turning into an urban experience. The urban program experience is a learning-centered program in which participating students and those in teacher preparation programs are given the first-hand experience with ethnically diverse students and prospective teachers under the supervision of well-trained and committed professionals, along with cooperative teachers, school administrators, and college professors. Through this comprehensive program with the community, participating students and teachers are provided with opportunities to get a better understanding of inner-city schools and, more importantly, gain a comprehensive experience that would enable them to teach more effectively, irrespective of his/her culture, socioeconomics, class, and other conceivable differences.

The program gave participants (pre-service) teachers and urban children the opportunity to collaboratively work with administrators, parents, teachers, and civic leaders from other universities. The program lasted for two weeks, but it had a meaningful impact on all participants, transforming and molding them into becoming culturally responsive practitioners. The program enabled students and prospective teachers to interact with one another in a manner that gave participants first-hand knowledge of the urban environment, contrary to the misconceptions they had developed from their closed communities. They were provided an opportunity to learn about one another.

The first-hand experience and the knowledge acquired from the urban experience completely transformed participants, as expressed in participants' comments during the interview, but before we get to that, let's spend a moment to illustrate with the diagram below the belief formation and modification process that helps to describe the journey of transformation participants experienced.

Belief Formation Diagram

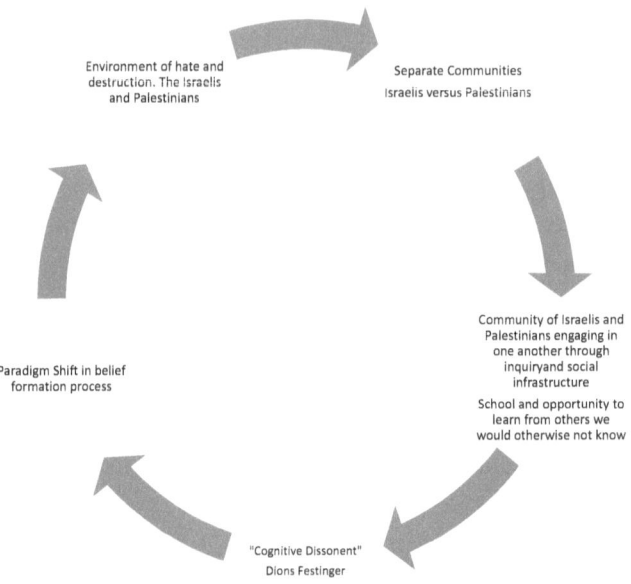

During the program, past and present urban graduates, pre-service teachers, administrators, teachers, and students were provided opportunities to work collaboratively with participants, including parents, civic leaders, and participants from various participating universities in cultivation of better understanding of people regardless of whether they were urban, suburban, or rural communities to realize the power of diversity and humanity in education. Below is the schedule of urban seminar program related activities. The program lasted for two weeks, and the activities were typically as follows:

Week 1 Starts the last day of Spring Semester

Monday

9:00 a.m.	Arrival, and Tour of the community
	Noon Luncheon, School Library
1:00 p.m.	Orientation Program, Auditorium

	Topic, Urban Education and Ogbota School Reform, Principal and Language Equity Issues Director
3:00p.m.	Tour of Schools
7:00p.m.	Icebreaker Activity Topic, Ethnography and Journal Writing Presenter, University Professor, Study Group Assignments, University

Tuesday

7:30 a.m.	First Day in Schools
3:30 p.m.	Community Service-Taller Puertorriqueno, 10th Street Snack
4:30 p.m.	Presenter- Tony Lake-Office of Curriculum Support School District of Ogbota
8:00 p.m.	Large Group Meeting "First Impression," University

Wednesday

7:30 a.m.	School Assignments
4:30p.m.	Workshop Session Topic, Stereotyping Minorities Presenter, Lisa Penn, University
7:00 p.m.	Learning Forum

Thursday

8:30 a.m.	School Assignments
3:30 p.m.	Workshop Session Topic-Multicultural Appreciation Presenters, Kim Onyeama and Miracle Ebony, Cultural Institute 20th Street
7:00 p.m.	Large Group Discussion of "An Asian Perspective, Wey, University

Friday

7:30 a.m.	School Assignments
3:30 p.m.	Group Project Meetings for Presentation
6:00 p.m.	Puerto Rican Experience Presenters, sr. Ngozi, Lorie Anderson, WCM Neighborhood Center
7: p.m.	Ethnic Food, Assignment of Group Projects for Saturday
8:30 p.m.	Tour of Historic Cultural Area

Saturday

9:00 a.m.	Service Learning Project Presenters, Sr. Ifeoma, Joyce Stanson, Location, WCM Neighborhood Center
12:00 Noon	Lunch
1:00 p.m.	Service Learning Projects
4:30 p.m.	Ethnic Meal and Traditional Music location, Community Garden at CM Square
8:00 p.m.	CM Cultural/ Entertainment Activities

Week 2

Sunday

7:30 a.m.	Optional Field Trips Student Group Selection
8:00 a.m.	Community Religious Options Location, First Baptist Church of Northville
2:00 p.m.	Tour of Central Mall Topic, "Using Primary Resources for Lesson Development" Presenter, Jim Timko Special Curriculum Coordinator School District of WCM

Monday

Memorial Day, Schools were Closed
            Tours of Historic and Cultural Areas

Tuesday

7:30 a.m.   School Assignments
4:30 p.m.   Teacher, Principal Panel
7:00 p.m.   Small Group Meetings for Group Presenters

Wednesday

7:30 a.m.   School Assignments
3:30 p.m.   Conflict Resolution Presenters. Ms. Laurie
                Johnson Uche, Former Student Teacher Komo
                High School Students-University
8:00 p.m.   Learning Forum

Thursday

7:30 a.m.   Last Day in Schools
7:30am   Group Presentations

Friday

7:00 a.m.   Checkout, University
12:00 Noon   Departure

One of the participating prospective teachers expressed her experience this way, "As result of my teaching experience at WCM school district, I have gained more insight on the plight of urban students and I therefore now have compassion towards students in an urban environment." The student continued, "Although I am familiar with a wide variety of research regarding urban education, no amount of research, reading, and classroom activities could have prepared me for the experience and knowledge I gained from the urban experience."

Another teacher candidate expressed his view. "I think the urban seminar should be compulsory for every student, particularly those in the teacher education program, because the program enables pre-service teachers to get a better understanding of their students from where they are to where the teacher ultimately wants to get the students. Everyone who wants to teach should consider the urban seminar experience."

The experience was certainly transformational. It clearly demonstrated that for us to truly transform our education, we must employ this unique teacher preparation program to prepare students with cross cultural training to enable them meet the needs of all students.

REFLECTION ON THE CHAPTER

As you finish reading the chapter, please reflect on how it resonates with you in the context of your past, present, and how the future looks. Please consider the past and your present experience as you proceed. As you think through those experiences, be specific as to how the chapter relates to your unique experience. Try to connect some of what you read to your own experience or the experience of other people that you know.

_____

_____

_____

_____

_____

_____

If you were able to relate or make connections, based on those connections you made, in what ways would you relay such powerful information to provide learning opportunities to others, especially young people?

_____

_____

_____

_____

_____

_____

In what ways has the content of this chapter helped you to ignite your metacognition while linking those experiences to multitudes of other experiences? As you reflect, please discuss how your experiences help foster meaningful understanding of the issues from one or more perspectives.

_____

_____

_____

_____

_____

_____

If you have no relatable experience, please feel free to express that too. The aim of this chapter is to keep engaging with one another in exploring these issues. We cannot solve these issues by isolating them or pretending that they don't happen.

_____

_____

_____

_____

_____

_____

CHAPTER 12

REFLECTION: IT EMBODIES COMMON EXPERIENCE

At the time of disruptions and divisions in our society, the question becomes, where do we go from here? To answer this big question, we need to take stock and reflect on our past and pay attention to the present. To undertake such a huge endeavor, we need to begin, first by answering the question of where we came from, and then, of course, where we have been in order to make a fruitful future decision as to where we go from here.

Clearly, America is made up of immigrants, and the word "immigrant" reminds us of who we are and where we came from. With exception of Native Americans – America's original people – all Americans directly or by extension came from different places, and we embody all continents. In the 16th and 17th centuries, people came to this land from many places, especially from European colonial countries to North America. They represented Europeans from different countries, such as British, Germans, Scandinavian, Czech, Finnish, etc. The European immigrants have been followed by other people from various corners of the earth, for instance, Asian Americans, including Filipinos, who were American colonial subjects after 1898, and migrated by the "tens of thousands" to Hawaii in the early 1900s. The first major wave of Asian immigration into the continental United States occurred primarily on the West Coast during the California Gold Rush, starting in the 1850s. They came in three different periods: 1849-1882, 1882-1965, and1965 to the present. The first period began shortly after the California Gold Rush and ended abruptly with the passage of the Chinese Exclusion Act of 1882.

Clearly, we all migrated from different places with unique circumstances and cultural backgrounds, some of which we lose and others we maintain. Others, however, we may not be able to change, even though that may be easier to somehow decrease the persistent oppression people go through for being different. In fact, sometimes some people can't even influence such changes even if they wanted to, in an effort to alleviate unbelievable pain and anguish they had to endure for being different. Additionally, for African Americans, it's difficult for them. Even today, they are still consistently subjected to unfair treatment in almost all areas of their lives, especially in the criminal justice system which we will get to in a moment. African Americans have gone and continue to go through painful experiences, including being discriminated against at workplaces, mortgage credit, even in elementary school, and especially in the criminal justice system. All these are in part due to their conspicuous skin pigmentation that they cannot change.

The extent to which we lose or retain our unique cultures determines the degree to which one could be engaged within the larger community, especially in some rural places like Ferguson, where one's skin pigmentation is a marker for so many terrible discriminatory behaviors, as documented by the Department of Justice Report on Ferguson. These cultural differences and the degree to which we lose or retain them explain the relative historical and cultural divisions in our society. The degree to which one loses or retains his or her culture is a function of controllable and uncontrollable factors and the degree to which one can be integrated into the community. In general, the controllable and uncontrollable factors significantly explain the divisions that are still apparent even in today's world. Although these divisions exist, some deny that they exist, and others pretend as if they do not exist. In order to overcome these divisions, we must accept that it exists. Denial or pretending that it does not exist will not remedy the situation. In fact, if anything, denial only helps people sweep it under the rug and thus exacerbate the thickness of such divisions. We must be united in acceptance that there are divisions and work together and thus get towards healing by confronting the factors that help create those divisions in the first place.

As we look at these historical divisions, for the purposes of this book, we will distinguish two perspectives: those who believe that we are a melting pot that includes all of us and the second who embrace divisions. The latter perpetuate the divisions as seen in their behaviors at creating a "we versus them" mentality.

History repeats itself. Clearly, this replication of history and subsequent lack of people mixing and understanding one another as Woodard pointed out to some extent remains with us. I completely concur with Woodward that the historical divisions along with cultural factors cumulatively influence current divisions in our society, as seen in our systemic discriminatory practices starting from our school system (urban and suburban), different communities (African American communities, Spanish communities, Asian American communities, and of course, the haves and the have nots communities). As explained in what Woodard characterized as a time of "little mixing in their settlement streams, as politics, religion, ethnic prejudice, geography, and agricultural practices that kept colonists almost entirely apart in four district tiers."

To some extent, we see the same in our local communities, which is a microcosm of our larger society, and to some extent, are still noticeable in education, religion, politics, economics, jobs, lending practices, and especially in our criminal justice system. These divisions are to some extent present in almost all aspects of our society. For instance, in our education system, after the landmark supreme Court ruling *Brown v Board of Education* outlawing segregation, some of our schools are still as segregated today as they were prior to the ruling in 1954. It's clear that our schools and how we operate in context of existing inequity in school funding by and large reflects our nation's inequity, in almost all aspects of our lives, into divisions such as black and white, and rich and poor, and in fact how we live and work in our communities and workplaces.

The fact is that we have not completely trusted one another, especially the older generations, and therefore, discrimination remains ubiquitous in our society. Although we are seeing some significant changes for better in terms of people mingling and connecting with people from cultures other than theirs, we still have a long way to go to truly eradicate the root causes of our divisions that are both overt and covert in nature. Perhaps one could argue that there are more covert forces driving the existing divisions and inequity in our society.

Clearly, as a society, we have not done enough to curb these divisions, and to reverse these divisions, we need to do a better job. To eliminate these divisions, we must commit to being more open and honest with each other about the issues driving it. If we are not open and honest in accepting the fact that we are not yet operating as one as evidenced in our school policies and practices and communities driven by one's zip code and political connections, among others, it will be difficult for us to convince outsiders to believe us when evidence of unfair practices in our criminal justice systems and job discrimination are still ubiquitous in our society.

In fact, we don't even have to go far to see evidence of what drives division and subsequently discriminatory practices in our society. It is pervasive, and even more prevalent in part because of our modern technology tools. Smartphones, for example, are helping to expose what people used to sweep under the rug and act as if it did not happen or outright deny that it ever happened, while the divisive "we versus them" mentality continues.

The division in our society is not new—it has been historical—and if something concrete is not done today, it will still be with us tomorrow. In her book, *The New Jim Crow*, Michelle Alexander painted a disturbing trend in our criminal justice, or injustice, system toward African Americans, a situation Charles Blow sited in the *New York Times*.[70]

In individual cases, some discourage their relatives, especially children, from mixing with others who are not like them, and sometimes we pretend

---

[70] Blow, Charles. 2012. "Opinion | Plantations, Prisons And Profits". *Nytimes.Com*. http://tinyurl.com/hrkox4p.

by saying positive things in public places and yet behave differently in private situations. This is particularly confusing to children because they can see the inconsistencies in how some adults provide public and private messages that are inconsistent and in fact contradictory. Some people have the tendency to say things that are not nice about others in private and yet say the opposite in public places. For instance, imagine a situation in which a well-known professional engaged in a discussion she characterized as "parents' dinner table discussion" – where some parents tend to develop a two-dimensional approach to dealing with the issue of race with the public and private approaches. While in public, they use deceptive mechanism to give the impression that they are friendly to people from different races or culture while in private they discourage their children from relating or becoming friends with people that are different from them.

This situation persists and certainly is evidenced in many aspects of our lives – inequity, discrimination, and lack of social justice for all – and some people live a lie to sustain hate and foster discriminatory practices against those that are not like them. This perplexing divisions and extended consequences of those acts continues. Unfortunately, this kind of behavior repeats itself and that is my concern, and we must break that unfortunate situation. However, if we do not have courageous leaders who would honestly step up and tackle the issues associated with inequality and unfair treatment of minorities, perhaps we won't be able to realistically address these issues. Let's look at the truth. If we truly want to deal with the truth, it would then mean that we must first accept the fact that racism and discrimination exist, and in fact it is ubiquitous in our society and we must also accept that it comes in different forms. With acceptance of these unfortunate situations, we must shift priorities to specifically set goals that would discourage racism and discriminatory practices while tackling the problem of structural inequality, discrimination, and lack of social justice that is pervasive in our society. Careful evaluation and analysis of what happens in our school system, specifically, discriminatory school practices, differential job opportunities, even towards people with similar qualifications, a situation a student of mine characterized this way, "It's no longer what you know that gets the bacon, it's whom you know that does the trick." If we are serious about perfecting this union, we must attack these issues of inequity that stem from the existing inequality. Clearly, if we intend to change and tackle the issues associated with bigotry, and its derivatives – discrimination and inequality – we must start with education that is devoid of structural racism ranging from preparation of teachers and administrators to meaningfully tackle persistent equity gaps that continue to remind us of the previous discriminations such as the one reflected by Judge Debra M. Brown when she pointed out in her ruling ordering Cleveland school district to desegregate it schools after five decades of litigation. We must fight to prevent what was evidenced in the past as a predictable result of a divided society.

Divisions and the Implications

In order to get a good sense of the issues that in one form or another are attributed to division and how they fuel even further divisions, we must learn to understand it in all its complex and complicated contexts. To that end, we will discuss so many dimensions of the contributing factors, such nationality, race, religion, etc. To understand these complex and complicated issues, we must investigate belief formation that influences why people do what they do. One's belief system is a function of the individual's collective internal and external experiences that include among others, family, cultures, race, religion, gender, ideation, and of course, new ideas that may stem from open engagement, and sharing different experiences and learning from each other's narratives. Factors that shape one's beliefs cumulatively provide the impetus for a broader-based inquiry and engagement with others via dialogue as we explore diversity and the implications for living in our rapidly shrinking global community, and it provides us the window through which we can learn the factors that may be contributing to our current circumstances as reflected by different groups.

African Americans and their Experiences

The discriminatory experience of African Americans occurs perhaps more frequently than any other racial group in this country, and to some extent. These experiences come in different forms, including individual or institutional. Institutional racism and discriminatory practices are those that come in form of laws, policies, institutions, and they are often linked to behaviors from individuals in positions of power. These are individuals who are by and large in control of making and executing laws, policies, or institutions that impact the lives of subordinates. Those activities shape how those who benefit or suffer as result of their decisions, and those cumulatively shape their varied individual or group perception of discriminatory practices.

The term "individual discrimination" is a form of racial discriminatory practice. Sometimes it's based on individual prejudice based on beliefs, cultures, and behavior toward African Americans and other groups. The evidence of institutional and individual discriminatory practices is obvious and mostly supported by federal, state government, and research organizations that research these issues. For instance, it's not often that United States Department of Justice investigates issues of racism and racial discriminatory practices, but recently, the Department of Justice studied discriminatory practices in three major cities in three American states. In each one of the three cities, the research turned out to reflect tremendous evidence of racial and discriminatory practices towards minorities, especially towards African Americans. Clearly, the evidence based on the investigations demonstrated the level of discriminatory experience minorities are subjected to in these cities and how it affects the victims' lives in general, especially in our criminal justice system, police mistreatment of minorities, in health, among other aspects that are well documented.

For example, in recent research designed to ascertain the perspective of victims of discriminatory practices, certain questions were posed, questions that focused on the experiences and perception of victims in their workplaces and how they felt about issues of social justice. Through the questions and answers, participants revealed their individual as well as group experiences. In one piece of research I studied, titled "Discrimination in America:

Experiences and views of African Americans scholars,[71] the scholars representing various organizations shed light on the issue of race and discrimination through question and answer sessions. The questions were designed to extract useful and hidden perspectives of diverse groups. They used well-designed questionnaires to extract valuable information, such as, "Do you believe you have ever personally experienced discrimination when applying for jobs because you are African American?"

In response to the above question, there were numerous responses telling unbelievable stories that African Americans endure at the workplace from hiring to promotions and the way they felt they were treated when compared to their counterparts, including whites and Asian Americans. Some of the questions and answers reflected phrases such as "because of their race" or "because they are Black."

Furthermore, in a 2017 study by NPR, the Robert Wood Johnson Foundation (RWJF), and the Harvard T.H. Chan School of Public Health illuminates reports from African Americans who shared their personal experiences with discrimination. The researchers' exploration of African Americans experiences via questions such as "How do African Americans experience discrimination in daily life?" In response to the questions, the researchers assert, "A new poll by NPR, the Robert Wood Johnson Foundation (RWJF), and the Harvard T.H. Chan School of Public Health illuminates reports from African Americans who share their personal experiences on discrimination. With unprecedented documentation, the poll covers a range of areas — from police interaction, to job applications, to health care, to racial slurs. This forum explored the poll results and their implications for a healthier, more equitable, and just society. This poll is the first among a series of reports that surveyed additional groups, including Latinos, Asian Americans, Native Americans, men, women, and LGBTQ adults, on their experiences with discrimination. This Forum event was presented on October 24, 2017, in collaboration with the Robert Wood

---

[71] Harvard T.H. Chan School of Public Health, Robert Wood Johnson Foundation and National Public Radio (NPR). 2017. Discrimination In America: Experiences And Views Of African Americans. Npr.Com. https://www.npr.org/assets/img/2017/10/23/discriminationpoll-african-americans.pdf

Johnson Foundation and NPR." The report clearly demonstrated that despite our feeling good after the election of President Obama, the first African American president, racial discrimination is still prevalent in our society, especially from the African American perspectives.[72] Following the incident was a further discrimination in our society, and a panel was engaged in discussion on the same issues moderated at Harvard University.[73]

According to the report, every group in America has faced discriminatory practices in our society, even the first Native Americans, but the level of discrimination African Americans had and continue to be faced with even on a contemporary basis is extensive. Clearly, each piece of research shows pervasive discrimination in our society, and it impacts African Americans in every aspect of their lives much more than any other race. These experiences help to explain what victims go through with extended consequences, including people's lives and premature deaths among others.

To say that the American judiciary system is inherently racist, as reflected by Michelle Alexander and the data stemming from Harvard research data showing that African Americans are four times more likely to be discriminated against than their white counterparts echoes the data that is reflected below.

Personal Experiences of Racial Discrimination among African Americans according to the Data from sources.[74]

---

[72] Harvard T.H. Chan School of Public Health, Robert Wood Johnson Foundation and National Public Radio (NPR). 2017. Discrimination In America: Experiences And Views Of African Americans. Npr.Com. https://www.npr.org/assets/img/2017/10/23/discriminationpoll-african-americans.pdf
[73] Harvard University. Discrimination in America: African American Experiences. YouTube.Com https://www.youtube.com/watch?v=8zX9CsxZh08
[74] Poll: Most Americans Think Their Own Group Faces Discrimination- Harvard and NPR Study written by Joe Neel NPR Deputy Senior Supervising Editor. https://www.npr.org/sections/health-shots/2017/10/24/559116373/poll-most-americans-think-their-own-group-faces-discrimination

Being paid or promoted equally	57%
Applying for jobs	56%
Interacting with police	50%
Trying to rent or buy a house	45%
Applying to or attending college	36%
Going to doctor or health clinic	32%
Trying to vote or participate in politics	19%

Unfair Treatment by the Police and the Court System[75]

Unfairly stopped or treated by police	60%
Unfairly treated by the courts	45%

African Americans Who Have Experienced Offensive Comments, Racial Slurs, or People Acting Afraid of Them Because of Their Race[76]

Offensive Comments	52%
Racial Slurs	51%
People Acting afraid of them	40%

---

[75] Ibid

[76] Ibid

Avoiding Activities Due to Concern of Racial Discrimination among African Americans[77]

Avoided calling police when in need	31%
Avoided Medical care	22%

The above data simply does not stand alone. The poll by NPR et al. illuminates firsthand reports from African Americans who share their personal experiences on discrimination. Clearly, these reports point to the same unequal treatment of certain segment of our citizens, and how such treatments influence their lives and how they respond to those treatments when their views are sought, and their collective point to the structural repetition that could be traced to the historical negativity directed towards African Americans. In fact, there is so much evidence to support this trend, such as awarding of loans showing that whites pay less than African Americans in terms of cost for loans, evidence of disproportionate discipline and suspension of kids in elementary schools for transgressions for which their white counterparts do not even get reprimands, among others.[78]

The issue of inequity in how people are treated ought to be seen in two dimensions—the individuals and the structural—and to combat this unfortunate situation, they should be tackled simultaneously. First, the perpetrator's policies and implications to the victims should be brought to light as the Pew and Harvard studies have done. Evidently, poor people have been treated poorly in part because they do not have the resources to lobby those in political positions to advocate and defend their interests. As a result, they are often intentionally or inadvertently mistreated through actions or inactions that negatively impact their lives, especially those in minority groups. These trends have affected how the victims feel. For example, it's now documented that the

[77] Ibid
[78] Harvard T.H. Chan School of Public Health, Robert Wood Johnson Foundation and National Public Radio (NPR). 2017. Discrimination In America: Experiences And Views Of African Americans. Npr.Com. https://www.npr.org/assets/img/2017/10/23/discriminationpoll-african-americans.pdf

fear of discrimination impacts how people feel.[79] For African Americans, they are fearful and feel that law enforcement officials discriminate in how they are treated. In fact, they believe that the whole criminal justice system treats them unfairly. As a result, they feel forced to design means through which to prevent that fear, including avoiding doing everyday activities because they don't trust police. We even see innocent black men being gunned down with the lame excuse that they thought the victims had guns. Clearly, these acts are by and large driven by fear. Police officers should be at minimum be made aware of how their behaviors are perceived by all those they were sworn to protect and defend. Furthermore, they should foster diversity and inclusivity to reverse these real or perceived horrible acts, and while at it, encourage police to deal with people as human beings to build relationships.

The History and Origin of Asian Immigration and Subsequent Discrimination They Endured in America.

Why did Chinese immigrants come to the US?

During the Gold Rush, labor was required and Asians were readily filling those job gaps. The difference between the Gold Rush period and now was that in those old days of the Gold Rush, there were more jobs than one could imagine and America was receptive to immigrants filling in those places. Today, even though there are jobs available, especially the low-level jobs, some people are not as receptive to immigrants as they were in those old Gold Rush days. In fact, there are some commonalities between the way the people felt as labor demand decreased during the middle of the Gold Rush. Just as we observe today, we have an administration that is going after desperate people, doing all they can to survive their economic circumstances, including immigrating to the United States. Clearly, the perception that these desperate people are coming to take our jobs is playing well politically and that's part of why our current administration is sending the military to the borders to prevent new immigrants from coming. Similarly, there were people during the Gold Rush days who, like people today, campaigned against Chinese immigrants and that led

---

[79] Ibid

politicians to enact what was known as the Chinese Exclusion Act. The Chinese Exclusion Act was designed as a response by some Americans' desire to prevent Chinese from going to California for the jobs available during the Gold Rush. The Chinese Exclusion Act was signed into law on May 6, 1882, by President Chester A. Arthur. This act was driven by people's pressure directed towards the government of the United States to halt Chinese immigration for ten years and prohibit them from becoming US citizens. Furthermore, they tried and successfully sustained it through the Geary Act of 1892. The law was extended for another ten years before becoming permanent in 1902. It is therefore important to realize that these discriminatory practices haven't just started now.

In order to understand the Asian American experience, one must become familiar with our history and certainly the historical exclusion in our immigration. The Chinese Exclusion Act was the first major law restricting immigration to the United States. It was enacted in response to economic fears, especially on the West Coast, where native-born Americans attributed unemployment and declining wages to Chinese workers, who they also viewed as racially inferior. Even though people no longer use the term "racial inferiority," my hunch is that there are still people who think that way, even though they feel inhibited to say it. If you are in doubt that some people think this way, just think about white supremacists and what they advocate.

The law was repealed by the Magnuson Act in 1943 during World War II, when China was an ally in the war against imperial Japan. Nevertheless, the 1943 act still allowed only 105 Chinese immigrants per year, reflecting persisting prejudice against the Chinese in American immigration policy. It was not until the Immigration Act of 1965, which was signed into law by President Johnson, which eliminated previous national-origins policy and thus allowed large-scale Chinese immigration to the United States after more than 80 years of restriction.

The immigration problems Asians faced were not limited to constraints via federal laws. People in various communities were facing other issues, which of course resulted in several responses, which included perceived or real challenge of demographics more than a century ago and continues to some degree to date as we will see momentarily. For instance, in addition to federal acts restraining the Asian immigrants, there were also local responses. The local San Francisco School Board reacted to immigrants by establishing a segregated Chinese Primary School for Chinese children to attend, including those who were American-born. In fact, by the turn-of-the century, after Japanese immigrants had settled in the wake of Chinese exclusion, certain school board superintendents employed all kinds of tactics to segregate Japanese, as the school superintendent, Aaron Altmann, advised the city's principals: "Any child that may apply for enrollment or at present attends your school who may be designated under the head of 'Mongolian' must be excluded, and in furtherance of this, please direct them to apply at the Chinese School for enrollment."[80]

Throughout their history, Asian Americans have confronted a long legacy of exclusion and inequity in relation to school policies and practices, particularly during periods of changing demographics, economic recession, or war. Despite the historic linguistic differences, Asian nationalities have been grouped together and treated as if they are the same in schools and in the larger society. The grouping of Asian Americans together, then, makes sense considering the historic links from the past to the present as I will be illustrating based on the kind of treatments people from Asian societies still receive because of the misconception that they are the same.

It's often said that the Asians who came to the United States escaped from war, social chaos, discrimination, and economic hardships among other reasons, but very little is said about their experience within American culture. Even though we talk about the past as if there is no similarity to present, in many ways, the past has some resemblance of the present as evidence in the mistreatment of Asians, which still lingers up to this day.

Racial experience of Asian Americans in our contemporary time still continues.

---

[80] Asian Americans Then and Now: Linking Past to Present. Asiasociety.Org. https://asiasociety.org/education/asian-americans-then-and-now

Despite what some people may say to suppress discriminatory practices that go on and on, such as: *There is no racism or discrimination, if there is any, I've yet to see or experience it.* The reason people make these periodic arguments could be either because they have not in fact been exposed to the discriminatory experience of others or perhaps its inconvenience makes some people choose the easy route – to ignore and pretend as if it never existed, and others resort to the rejection of inconvenient truth; that of discriminatory practices others endure. Despite the obvious denial of discriminatory practices in our society, the fact remains that anyone who lives and reads about the collective experience of our diverse communities, one would say there is no evidence of discriminatory practices of some sort, otherwise, the person may be in denial because no one that lives in our society could possibly escape conscious or unconscious mistreatment of people in our contemporary time.

We clearly can no longer deny the historical policies and practices of discrimination in our society, but it's equally important that we accept the fact that despite our nation's progress, a lot of people still experience discriminatory practices. With the study of history, people should realize that although there is still evidence of racism and subsequently discrimination, although it's not close to what people endured in the past. If you really conduct basic research on racism and racial discrimination, you will be surprised the extent of racism and discrimination in the past, and then fast forward, you still see evidence of racism and racial discrimination and how people could be addressing it. For instance, when the Deputy Metro Editor for the *New York Times* Michael Luo experienced racial discrimination from a woman who yelled at him and his family and essentially told them to go home, it was not fun and games for Luo's family. Imagine being an American and yet some other American perceives you as not being an American and yells at for you and your family to go home, telling you that you don't belong here. This is in fact what the Deputy Metro Editor of the *New York Times* had to endure with his family, and the only reason why most people know about his family experience was essentially because he had a platform and courage to share what happened to him and his family, as we will see in a moment. However, how about John Doe with a similar experience with neither a platform nor the courage to share?

REFLECTION ON THE CHAPTER

As you finish reading the chapter, please reflect on how it resonates with you in the context of your past, present, and how the future looks. Please consider the past and your present experience as you proceed. As you think through those experiences, be specific as to how the chapter relates to your unique experience. Try to connect some of what you read to your own experience or the experience of other people that you know.

_____

_____

_____

_____

_____

_____

_____

If you were able to relate or make connections, based on those connections you made, in what ways would you relay such powerful information to provide learning opportunities to others, especially young people?

_____

_____

_____

_____

_____

_____

_____

In what ways has the content of this chapter helped you to ignite your metacognition while linking those experiences to multitudes of other experiences? As you reflect, please discuss how your experiences help foster meaningful understanding of the issues from one or more perspectives.

_____

_____

_____

_____

_____

_____

If you have no relatable experience, please feel free to express that too. The aim of this chapter is to keep engaging with one another in exploring these issues. We cannot solve these issues by isolating them or pretending that they don't happen.

_____

_____

_____

_____

_____

_____

CHAPTER 13

CONTEMPORARY DISCRIMINATORY PRACTICES IN AMERICA

Clearly, we could not document all the daily experiences of what ordinary people go through in our society, especially minorities in rural America. However, occasionally, we are provided windows through which to imagine what people go through on a daily basis, and sometimes, the extended consequences to families and what they endure. All these experiences should remind us that we are not treating all our people as some may think, as it was revealed by Mr. Luo and his family experience.

Mr. Luo and his family are prominent American citizens, and yet, they were harassed and told to go home because of how they appeared in their community in New York, a place considered to be progressive. If it happened in New York, you can only imagine what happens in rural communities, such as in Missouri and Mississippi among others, states where we have heard stories of despicable acts, including hanging human beings because of the pigmentation of their skin. The kind of stories some would characterize as historical, and yet we were reminded of our historical experience as if it were yesterday, when a United States Senator was caught by *Washington Post* writers Michael Brice-Saddler and Deanna Paul on video saying in public, "If he invited me to a public hanging, I'd be in the front row."[81] The same comment that captured Senator Hyde-Smith was heard on Twitter posted by journalist and blogger Lamar White Jr. When Mike Espy, Democratic senatorial candidate, was asked to respond, he simply said he does not know what was in the senator's heart, but he knows what came out of her mouth. It was not nice, but more revealing information that aligns with the senator's comment are coming along. According to a report in the *Jackson Free Press* and reference by Thinkprogress.org, it pointed out that "Sen. Cindy Hyde-Smith (R-MS) sent her daughter to a private school that was established to allow white parents to avoid sending their children to the same schools as Black children, after Hyde-Smith graduated from a similar school in the 1970s."[82]

Back to Mr. Luo and his family's experience, it was obviously an annoying experience for Mr. Luo and his family, who are American citizens. However, Luo did not go quietly like most people who experience such indignation in our society. Instead, Mr. Luo responded by writing an open letter to the woman who yelled and embarrassed him and his family. Mr. Luo's letter generated a lot publicity and subsequently propelled thousands of Asian Americans to respond through sharing of their varied experiences with racial prejudice. It was an eye opener to someone who could not believe that it happens in their community.

The incident generated a lot of questions, some of which are as follows:

- What can be done to address the issue of racial discrimination?
- What kind of response would be appropriate for these kinds of incidents?
- And is there a path forward?

These were some of the questions.

---

[81] Forgery Quint, and James Arkin. 2018. "Mississippi Newspaper: Hyde-Smith Attended Segregation Academy". *POLITICO*. https://tinyurl.com/y8nb6ojx.

[82] Ressler, Tara Culp. 2018. "Cindy Hyde-Smith sent her daughter to a private school created to help white kids bypass integration". *Thinkprogress.Org* https://thinkprogress.org/cindy-hyde-smith-segregation-academy-daughter-mississippi-d1fec8c9c0e6/

In response to the above questions, a *New York Times* journalist, experts of Asian descent, and readers engaged in a live chat on the issue. Below are just a few excerpts from professionals who participated in that enlightened discussion, and you can of course watch the entire video that reflects bias so many had and continue to experience up to now in 2019. You can check the full story via their video. [83]

As you can see, this was professionally done and most of those involved are professionals, and as you follow their discussions, you will find out that racism or racial prejudicial judgment of people based on all kinds of misconceptions people may have is ubiquitous in our society, even amongst the Asian American community.

In this discussion that stemmed from Michael Luo's experience, which he channeled as a learning moment, we can see clearly that so many people still experience overt and covert discriminatory practices, as evidenced in some of their responses during their engagement.

During that occasion, Mr. Luo, Deputy Metro Editor of the *NYT*, and the person who brought the issue to light, they moderated the discussion, which fostered meaningful engagements and below are few of the excerpts that generated serious discussions.

Mr. Luo began by thanking everyone for joining the conference. He said, "I'd love to start by asking everyone to reflect a little about what has unfolded over the last week after I posted my open letter. The response has been extraordinary. I'm curious what everyone else's take has been on it. Is this an Asian-American moment?" Although the actual transcript is public, I will only provide brief excerpts selected from the engaged discussions to give readers a sense of what people still go through in our society for being different.

---

[83] Luo, Michael. 2016. "Confronting Racism Against Asian-Americans". *Nytimes. Com* https://www.nytimes.com/interactive/2016/10/17/us/asian-american-confronting-racism.html

Japanese Americans were told to "prove their loyalty" by quietly going to camps during World War Two, for example. Of course, many were not quiet then. And Asian American activism and protest have always been part of our history. But I think that Asian Americans – especially younger Asian Americans – are more vocal and active in calling attention to inequality and discrimination in all of its forms today.

FROM A READER

Asian-Americans, especially those of the first generation, are often detached from the political process that so often drives visibility and conversation in this country. In addition, because of cultural aspects, involvement in politics is often discouraged. How would Asian-Americans who want to be involved in politics best approach it (e.g., working for politicians that best represent interests of the Asian-American community, running for office, encouraging voter turnout), despite current obstacles?

Michael Luo, Deputy Metro Editor, *NYT.* Discrimination based on the Asian experience are numerous, including of others. Other cultural groups go through similar experience.

The story of immigrants in the United States is not new, and the more we research, the more we learn. For instance, James Estrin's article titled "Race/Related" on Saturday 17, 2018, he referenced and quoted a Chinese librarian. "The Chinese have been in the Delta for more than a hundred years," and he continued, "When we came initially, we didn't have rights. We couldn't go to the white schools, couldn't get a haircut or go to the hospitals. We were second-class citizens. After the Civil Rights era, we gained more rights. I think the communities realized, "Hey, the Chinese are really contributing." According to James Estrin, Ms. Quon was among a dozen Mississippians of Chinese descent who were photographed and interviewed by Andrew Kung and Emanuel Hahn. The two Chinese Americans, like every other ethnic group, were interested in their history. Besides Asians, other groups have their own experiences, including the Jews and their relationships with African Americans.

Jewish American Experience

I read the disturbing news of the divisions, charges, and counter charges between the African American poor community and the Jewish members of the community in the District of Columbia. Do these people know how African Americans and the Jewish community leaders worked together for equity and social justice for all during our nation's very difficult time in the past? I doubt it. Therefore, both sides need strong leaders who must rekindle that sense of oneness and commitment to equity and social justice for all. As they work on assembling such leaders, they must ensure anyone who tries to exploit this unfortunate situation for political or economic gains is excluded.

Instead of the apparent divisions, this is the time for them to unite and fight a common enemy, poverty and racism, while striving for a better and united African American and Jewish community. I would suggest that those in leadership positions should consider inviting Dr. Cornel West and the guy he often addressed as his Jewish brother to come and tell both the African American and the Jewish people their history of working together, especially those in leadership. Cornel West's message, I am sure, will be along the lines of "knock it off, come together, and work together for the beloved city in the Hill; that's what DC should represent and that what those in leadership should strive for."

Regardless of what form the misunderstanding takes, those in leadership positions must step up and unite African Americans and the Jewish members of the community so that they can, together, strive for a more understanding and unified community while working on continuous engagement with one another in their effort to cultivate a better tomorrow.

Hispanic American Experience

There is abundant evidence being pointed out by researchers that the extent of discrimination and unfair treatment of Americans who are perceived to be members of minority groups is immense. There is clearly evidence of discrimination and unfair treatment of minorities, especially African

Americans and Hispanics in our society. The most recent investigation of the department of justice in three communities and in three different states has shone light on the level of discriminatory and unfair treatment of Americans who are perceived by other Americans as the "others."

My focus on this piece is to provide the rationale for leaders, including those in the public and private organizations, to realize and understand the urgency required in dealing with these issues of discrimination and mistreatment of our people. I would bypass the historical and discriminatory practices, except when it adds value to the urgency of leaders' ability to do the work that must be done if we intend to keep republic as we were reminded in the notes of Dr. James McHenry, one of Maryland's delegates of the 1787 convention.

Like African Americans, Latinos have suffered extensively from their experiences of being treated unfairly as a result of misconceptions people may have about them. The range of suffering as a result of discriminatory practices is immense. In his piece, Joe Neel, a member of NPR's award-winning health and science team, who directs the coverage of breaking news in health and science, ranging from disease outbreaks and advances in medical research to debates over health reform and public health, asserted that Latinos experience racial and unfair treatment in our society.

In furtherance of discriminatory experience of minorities in American society, there is clear evidence that minorities, including, of course, Hispanics, experience acts of discrimination in many ways. Jens Manuel Krogstad and Gustavo Lopez pointed out that about half of Hispanics in the U.S. (52%) say they have experienced discrimination or have been treated unfairly because of their race or ethnicity, according to a newly released report by Pew Research Center survey on race in America.

Hispanics' experience with discrimination or being treated unfairly varies greatly by age. Among Hispanics ages 18 to 29, 65% say they have experienced discrimination or unfair treatment because of their race or ethnicity. By comparison, only 35% of Hispanics who are 50 or older say the same – a 30-percentage-point gap. In addition, according to the Pew

Research Center survey, Hispanics born in the U.S. (62%) are more likely than immigrants (41%) to say that they have experienced discrimination or unfair treatment. There are also differences by race. For example, 56% of nonwhite Hispanics say this has happened at some point in their lives, a higher share than that among white Hispanics (41%). Hispanics are significantly less likely than blacks (71%) to say they have experienced discrimination or unfair treatment due to their race or ethnicity at some point in their lives, a gap that extends across most demographic subgroups, including gender and education. With this trend, I would conclude that most minorities have experienced some sort of discrimination in our society, as we will see in a moment when we have a look at Muslim Americans.

Muslim American Experience

As for Muslims coming to the United States, many historians have claimed that the earliest Muslims to arrive in the United States came from Africa and Spain, and as a result, they made their way to Caribbean and Gulf of Mexico. In fact, there were reports suggesting that during Christopher Columbus' journey to the new world, he came with a book written by Portuguese Muslims who had come to the New World in the 12th Century. There were others who claimed that there were Muslims, some of whom were notable, including a man named Istafan, who was characterized as having accompanied the Spanish as a guide to the new world during the early part of the 16th century to the United States. In their conquest of what became Arizona and New Mexico, they arrived in significant numbers, with so many settling in Ohio, Michigan, Iowa, and the Dakotas, among other places.[84]

These Muslim immigrants in many ways were like most immigrants from other places to America. They were seeking greater economic opportunities than what their homeland offered, and by and large, they worked like most other immigrants; often, they did manual labor related jobs. In fact, one of the first big employers of Muslims and blacks was the Ford Company, and these were often the only people willing to working the hot, difficult conditions of

---

[84] Islam in America. PBS Org. http://www.pbs.org/opb/historydetectives/feature/islam-in-america/

the factories in those days, and that remains one of the reasons why there are many Muslims, especially the African American presence, in Michigan area up to this time. That also could explain the existence of the strong African American Muslim nationalist movement that still exists to this day.

In fact, there are different estimates when it comes to the number of American Muslims in the country. The American Muslim Council claims 5 million, while the non-partisan Center for Immigration Studies believes the figure is closer to 3 or 4 million followers of Islam. The American Religious Identification Study by the City University of New York, compiled in 2001, put the number of Muslims at 1,104,000.

Historical figures such as Malcolm X and Muhammad Ali contributed to the elevation of Muslim to public prominence, and those among others resulted in the establishment of over 1500 Islamic centers and mosques around the country, a number that has increased substantially. It is believed that Islam is the second largest religion in America. Since the attacks of 9/11, prejudice against Muslims has risen sharply and that continues to be the case, especially after Obama's administration, and that may explain why Muslims are responding by being more active in the political process, striving to educate their neighbors about their religion, history, and yes, even culture.

Throughout this book, we have explored the issues associated with diversity, and now having gained the knowledge of what being different means and how such differences could either be real or perceived could be interpreted differently both by the victim or perpetrators, and more importantly, that we are in a society that in spite of some misdeeds, is the best in the world in terms of from people from various cultures. It is important that we have quality leaders to help shape a better society where the value of equity and social justice for all and that appreciates diverse cultures. I submit that in meeting all this, quality leadership is essential.

The Need for Leadership on Issues of Diversity

Leadership means being a visionary and seeing beyond what an average person can see and conceptualize. Leadership means having the vision, goal, and plan of action and appropriately implementing strategies that not only prevent foreseeable problems in the future, but more importantly, be able to lead the subordinate to a successful outcome.

In order to experience a successful outcome in any initiative, leaders must learn to ask critical questions, such as when we say that things are not going as they should, we must be clear as to the specific things that are not going as they should. Let's take, for instance, for a teacher to say that students act out; acting out is too generalized. One must pose the right question, such as, what does acting out mean or what action constitutes acting out?

In one of the cases I had read, the principal of a school saw a bunch of students and asked whether they knew that what they were doing constituted an act that was problematic, and further drilled to specifics that crystalized what an action that constituted a problem was and why they must avoid it at all costs.

To engage students in what some will characterize as an active involvement of the learner in the process, the students were asked to list actions they would take to address issues or problems. As they listed actions they planned to take, they were further asked what they would do if their strategy did not work. What happened? Could you tell me what else you could do to ameliorate the situation? Could you tell me a time you got into the problem areas? Shortly after such engagements, the question was posed: what happens when there is a problem? One responded, "We get suspended, and depending on the magnitude of the problem, one could get expelled." The leader said, "I don't give out suspensions because it does not work; instead, it exacerbates the problem." She proceeded to say, "Work together with others to get to a better solution or make better decisions."

Like in every area of life's journey, in diversity, I encourage leaders to focus on leadership because leadership is central to success on issues of diversity; and to succeed, they present examples of what their goals are and how to achieve them. They could begin by visualizing their goals and clarifying strategies to achieve whatever goals they want to accomplish.

It does not matter what people do or what they want to achieve in school or in the workplace. They also must consider the resources, including the time for them to achieve the expected goal or result. Of course, society deals with troublemakers or other related issues differently.

In the case of the students who got in trouble with the principal, nobody seemed to have the answer, then one started to explain that each time someone fails, the society builds new jails. One student responded, "I remember of a time my friend got into trouble, he got into two problems. In the first instance, he was told by his teacher to get out of class instead of going to the principal's office. On the second occasion, he was involved in making noise and was suspended."

Diverse experiences that stem from how our varied belief systems are formed, and the imagined work that must be done to ensure that everyone is respected and that we have enough forums to learn instead of consistently sweeping the problem under the rug or outright denial that it does not happen here. I do not care where you live, or what you think, especially when you are part of the group that sweeps the issues under the rug or deny that it happens where you are. I want to be loud and clear, and please believe me, because every other person that is a citizen here like you would not tolerate this nonsense, just as I know that if you are treated the way you treat those whose identity is unclear to you, you wouldn't like it.

Although I am currently focusing on fellow citizens, I must say, that even when someone is not part of us, you should never treat your fellow human being in a different way than you would like to be treated. Ask your fellow Americans who are in various parts of the world, how do they get treated? If they respond along the line of fairness or in a manner that reflects the "Golden Rule Principle" (treating people how you would like to be treated) ask them whether that is how they treat others. Foreigners are human beings too, and why don't you treat these foreigners in a similar way that all Americans in their countries are treated by their citizens?

This incident is not the only time we experience this kind of mistreatment on basis of others; it's sad, but it happens. Every so often, we hear, observe, or read about actions motivated by factors such as racism, socioeconomic, religion, sexual orientation, and political ideology, among others. While there are people who never experience mistreatment whether it's based on race, class, or religion, as we have seen in recent years with reference to how the Muslim people are often mistreated, we must accept that although we may not be experiencing these terrible incidents, we must understand that for some people, this is what they experience every day, and in some cases, multiple times a day. You, therefore, must not criticize until you walk in their shoes. In fact, I encourage you to help them overcome the anguish these victims are subjected to on a daily basis and lend your support to the victim. No one deserves to be going through what the victims go through, not once, not twice, but in some cases, these are the daily experiences of some people who go through this kind of anguish.

These kinds of behaviors are being reported in all aspects of our society's lives. As one episode ends, another begins. It's like a never-ending story that continuously fuels the cultivation of seeds of rancor, and subsequently divides our society between parties based on issues associated with isms, such as race, gender, socioeconomics, and nationality among others. These are difficult and complex issues that are often denied by some and simplified by others, which cumulatively continue to contribute to the creation of an even bigger division amongst people in our society.

What has our world become? What informs our belief system, and why does our belief system propel us to do what we do? These are some of the questions we have explored in this book, which will in turn be reflected throughout the remaining part of the book with a focus on solutions.

Clearly, these behaviors happen, and it depends on a number of factors that ultimately could be attributed to whether it's good, bad, or neutral behaviors, and as we explore the factors that influence these behaviors, we will ultimately provide recommendations that while sustaining the belief systems that foster good behaviors – or positive experiences as to how we should treat one another. On the other hand, and perhaps more importantly, we will equally explore the factors that foster negative behaviors, and ultimately, deconstruct those belief systems that propel us to mistreat our fellow human beings and ultimately reconstruct a belief system that embraces Golden Rule principles (treating others how we would want to be treated).

Before we go further, it's worthy of note and emphasis that I might add here that our belief system is the core driver of our behavior; and that remains the case regardless of whether it's good or bad behavior. Before we get to the description of individual or group experiences and good or bad driven behaviors, let us spend some time exploring and understanding the process of belief formation, because one's belief cannot be divorced from the person's behavior. Our belief system is by and large the function of our experience, environment, culture, values, and our social institutions, such as the church, school, and the environment.

One's behavior is always driven by the individual's belief. Despite the pervasive nature of the problems that subsequently morph into behaviors from overt to covert discrimination, certain elements of our society are still in denial of some of our discriminatory behaviors. Our founding fathers realized that certain aspects of our systems were unfair and inconsistent, as indicated in the phrase they evoked in the opening of the United States Declaration of Independence that states among others: "We hold these truths to be self-evident, that all men are created equal, that they are endowed by their Creator with certain unalienable rights that among these are life, liberty, and the pursuit of happiness."

They knew that the phrase they purported to mean – equality and fair treatment of all – was not the case for all, and as we fast forward to the present, those are wonderful words, but they are still not real for so many of our citizens, especially for those who are poor and particularly African Americans, who continuously experience terrible treatment in almost every aspect of our system. Clearly, these wonderful words are great, but in reality, one must be blind or in denial not to see it false; it did not apply to either blacks or women or Hispanic Americans. That's perhaps why the founders urged us to work towards a more perfect union because they realized that those beautiful words did not apply to all. I believe that we will someday perfect this union by making those words apply to all regardless of gender, race, sexual orientation etc. The hope that we will one day perfect the envisioned union motivated me to pose a question whose answer would enable us to explore why despite all these years and efforts to perfect this union; we continue to have all kinds of challenges. This is the main theme covered in this book. Every now and then, some people experience discrimination in schools, in their jobs, and in our criminal justice system, among other areas.

I would argue that the main reason why we have not been able to tackle the problem of inequity and all the issues associated with it could be explained by our balkanized society stemming from what I characterized elsewhere as "artificial walls." If you like, call it "invisible walls" that demarcate groups (black and white, rich and poor, educated and uneducated, privileged and less privileged, the haves and the have nots), which thus prevent people from mixing and knowing one another and how they may have contributed in the cultivation of "them versus us" belief systems. I would argue that those divergent beliefs continue to divide us and thus shape our different mindsets that often manifest in behaviors between those in confined artificial walls and those outside. We will be sharing examples momentarily, but before we do, let's examine the issues that cumulatively shape one's belief system and how such belief systems drive one's behavior, and how such a belief system could be changed or transformed.

A Belief System that Drives Behavior and How It's Formed

As we deepen our effort to better understand the complex nature of human behavior and the belief system that informs those behaviors, we would explore and highlight certain elements that influence belief formation, which once framed, drives behavior as well as explores the process of belief transformation (later).

Let us begin by exploring the formation of belief system.

Belief Formation

What informs our behavior as an individuals or groups? What has our world become? What informs our belief system, and why does our belief system propel us to do what we do? Those are some of the questions we are going to explore in this section, which will in turn be reflected throughout the drama associated with human differentiated behaviors. Clearly, there are good and bad behaviors, and as we explore the factors that influence these behaviors, we will ultimately provide recommendations that while sustaining the belief systems that foster good behaviors – that reflect positively on how we treat one another, but more importantly, we will equally explore the factors that foster negative behaviors, and ultimately, deconstruct those belief systems that propel us to mistreating our fellow human beings and ultimately reconstruct a belief system that embraces Golden Rule principles (treating others how we would want to be treated).

Our belief system is the core driver of our behavior, and that remains the case regardless of whether it's good or bad behavior, as demonstrated with the diagram below. Our belief system is by and large the function of our experience, environment, culture, values, and our institutions, such as churches and schools, etc.

Belief Formation Diagram.

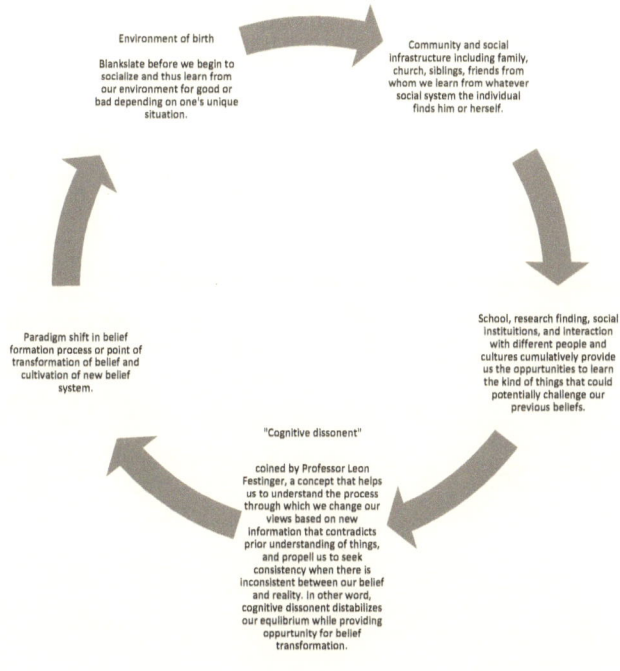

Environment of birth

Blankslate before we begin to socialize and thus learn from our environment for good or bad depending on one's unique situation.

Community and social infrastructure including family, church, siblings, friends from whom we learn from whatever social system the individual finds him or herself.

School, research finding, social instituitions, and interaction with different people and cultures cumulatively provide us the oppurtunities to learn the kind of things that could potentially challenge our previous beliefs.

Paradigm shift in belief formation process or point of transformation of belief and cultivation of new belief system.

"Cognitive dissonent"

coined by Professor Leon Festinger, a concept that helps us to understand the process through which we change our views based on new information that contradicts prior understanding of things, and propel us to seek consistency when there is inconsistent between our belief and reality. In other word, cognitive dissonent distabilizes our equilibrium while providing oppurtunity for belief transformation.

The above diagram demonstrates and summarizes the process through which we accumulate values, experiences, and norms that interact and are infused into the formation of one's belief system. One's belief system is a function of the individual's collective internal and external experiences that include, among others, family, cultures, race, religion, gender, and ideation. Going back to Mark Twain's assertion of "where you live really does shape who you are" as well as Ibn Khaldun's reminder that the rise or decline of human interaction with external and internal conditions shapes one's belief, and similarly, Karl Marx's sentiment that men make their own history but outside the condition of their choosing, I concur with their statements, especially when we think of children, because they do not have control of who their parents are or the community in which they live or even as to whether they should have siblings. This is evident in the case of China until the latter part of 2016, when they reversed law limiting how many children Chinese could have. However, for adults, positions on factors that shape one's belief provides the impetus for deeper and broad-based inquiry, and engagement with others via dialogue as we explore diversity and the implications for living in our rapidly shrinking global village.

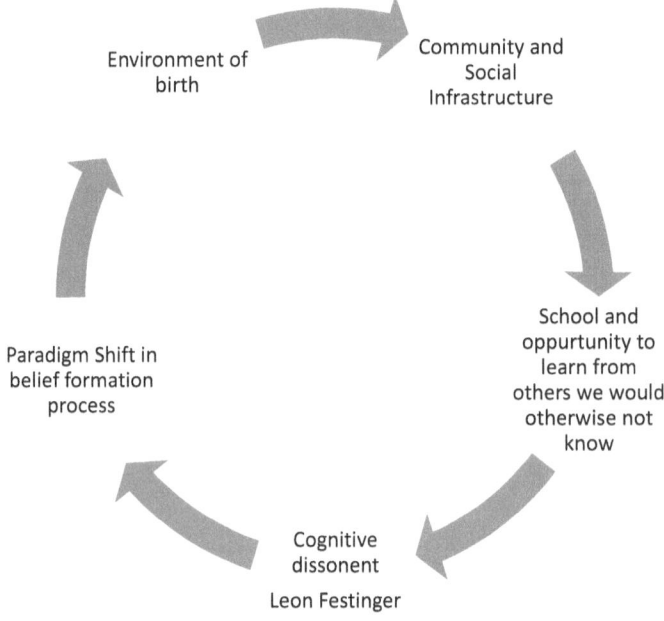

One's observed experiences, materials read regardless of whether they are in the past or present, cumulatively continue to shape one's belief system, which in turn influences how one behaves, as would be evidenced in the examples that will be brought into the discussion momentarily. In order to understand one's belief system, one must become familiar with the cultural values, biases, and institutions that cumulatively shape one's belief. Human beings construct their belief system mostly from the experiences and the company they keep. Each society or individual within the society has culturally specific knowledge of his or her group, and that specific knowledge combines to shape one's belief system. For one to truly understand other people, the individual must have to first understand him or herself by genuinely asking honestly and responding to the questions below:

1. Who am I?
2. Why do I think or act the way I do?
3. What factors influence my belief system?

You can begin by reflecting on your experiences from childhood with your siblings, parents, and the entire members of your community or the company you keep. Your relationship with them cumulatively factors into one's belief system.

Imagine experiencing what so many Muslims people go through by what you read, observe, and hear: stories of mistreatment of people based on the perception that they are Muslims, and then comes a firsthand experience in which you need to assume the following. Assume that you are a Muslim woman flying from Chicago to a Washington airport and while the attendant was giving drinks, asking their preferences and meeting those preferences. It's now your turn, and you proceed to ask for a can of coke that is not opened for hygienic reasons, and you are told no, then the next person after you requests for an unopened can just as you did, no questions asked, and the person gets it. Also, assume that you have been experiencing other discriminatory practices similar to those that are reported on a daily basis related to humiliation. It's like a never-ending story stemming from conscious and unconscious bias that is being dramatized in real time. The difference this time is that it is no longer unconscious bias; it's a deliberate attempt to humiliate you and let you know that you can be treated without respect. How would you feel?

Now keep in mind differential treatment that goes on every day in our society. Well, depending on the level of negative experiences, you will to some degree read it differently and may in fact either act very angrily or mildly, depending on whether you bring other disturbing patterns of mistreatment into the equation. If you have had varied experiences, it will be reflected accordingly and perhaps one may act angrily, depending on different circumstances. It's not always the victim alone that suffers. Others, including the victimizers in certain situations, unexpectedly suffer too.

Imagine being a member of the group perceived to be perpetuating discriminatory practices toward the Muslim people. How would you feel? Let it settle, and then think of you having to be in the midst of people that see you as an oppressor and attribute all that happens to them to your action. How do you feel about the situation and how would you expect them to act towards you? Finally, think about the scenarios that could be unleashed should you switch positions. Describe how you would react in each switched position. If you do it right, you will feel the pain on both sides.

Similarly, imagine the experiences of other people, especially those who suffer every day for what others gloss over as if nothing happened. Examples include being mistreated because of your race, your gender, your nationality, your ideas or whether you are a liberal or conservative.

Imagine being an African American being at the Starbucks incident in Philadelphia where police officers were called upon and they actually came and arrested you in handcuffs while people at the store were asking them and implying that it was unfair and yet the police still took you in handcuffs, humiliated and perhaps injured you with their handcuffs among other pain and suffering you endured.[85]

---

[85] Associated Press. 2018. Black men arrested at Philadelphia Starbucks feared for their lives. *The Guardian*. https://www.theguardian.com/business/2018/apr/19/starbucks-black-men-feared-for-lives-philadelphia

On one hand, you heard the emphatic call from reasonable people in their efforts to address the issue, such as the President of Starbucks did by meeting with the Mayor of Philadelphia and assuring the black community that such incidents should not happen and certainly will not happen again. Furthermore, the President of Starbucks apologized to the victim, and in addition, he set May 29th as a day to train all his employees on issues of conscious and unconscious bias. Clearly the Starbucks president understands the pain and anguish victims went through his actions.

Contrast the Starbucks president's action to that of those who consistently blamed the victim like Bob Barr in his piece in the Town Hall that attracted my attention on Twitter when I posted, "It's unconscionable that former congressman Bob Barr is criticizing courageous leaders like Howard Schultz for addressing conscious and unconscious bias through employees' training at Starbucks." Followed by another of my posting, "If anything, those who purport to be leaders like Bob Barr should be working to eradicate bias instead of critiquing courageous people like Howard who do."

Similarly, imagine being a Lesbian American, and experiencing discriminatory behavior like being denied services where everyone else is provided services. Of course, you are a victim of discrimination. Similarly, imagine being a white lady discriminated and bypassed for promotion because of your gender; obviously you are a victim of gender discrimination. It is the same if you are a Latino and are bypassed for promotion, you are a victim of discrimination. Similarly, imagine being a mixed-race child and you are discriminated against by an ignorant teacher. You are a victim whether it's conscious or unconscious discrimination. It's discrimination and the victim endures some sort of pain and anguish whenever it occurs.

Based on the above, imagine being able to switch your code from one of the above and are able to experience each individual's experience based on their various situations, perhaps those experiences and your ability to shift codes will put you in a unique position to understand the pain and anguish people from different backgrounds endure when the act of discrimination occurs regardless of one's situation.

This is where engagement of people who may not agree with each other could yield better outcomes, but it rarely happens because of leaders like Bob Barr. We need more leaders like Mr. Johnson, President of Starbucks. We also need such leaders like Johnson in all areas of leadership if we are ever going to solve our real problems. It is of great importance that we widen the company we keep to include those who are different from us, and while we do so, we must also listen and learn from one another to do better in all areas of human endeavor in a fair way that reflects diversity and inclusion in our organization or work.

In a piece by Eric Levenson, Paul Murphy, and Giantned, a New York Attorney who is historically known for his racist rants and confrontation of minorities, this attorney was once reported to be "harassing people who appeared to be foreigners." "You are not a citizen, you are not. You are an ugly foreigner." He was further characterized as one who berated employees and customers for speaking Spanish in a New York City cafe. Further evidence revealed that the same lawyer had a history of confronting people he perceived to be berating others, even citizenship. This individual may have done all that might have been uncovered, but we must look at what contributed to shaping such an individual to what he has become.

As we go back and forth, we must see other things, such as an enraged individual minding her business and suddenly someone secretly calling the police on her. Police actually came and started asking for an ID and the woman screamed at the police, "Why do I need to give you my ID? What did I do?" The officer said because police were called and the woman shouted back. Perhaps more engagement and striving for understanding of one another in every context of diversity could help reduce or better yet, eradicate all forms of discriminatory practices that are prevalent in our society.

REFLECTION ON THE CHAPTER

As you finish reading the chapter, please reflect on how it resonates with you in the context of your past, present, and how the future looks. Please consider the past and your present experience as you proceed. As you think through those experiences, be specific as to how the chapter relates to your unique experience. Try to connect some of what you read to your own experience or the experience of other people that you know.

_____

_____

_____

_____

_____

_____

If you were able to relate or make connections, based on those connections you made, in what ways would you relay such powerful information to provide learning opportunities to others, especially young people?

_____

_____

_____

_____

_____

_____

In what ways has the content of this chapter helped you to ignite your metacognition while linking those experiences to multitudes of other experiences? As you reflect, please discuss how your experiences help foster meaningful understanding of the issues from one or more perspectives.

_____

_____

_____

_____

_____

_____

If you have no relatable experience, please feel free to express that too. The aim of this chapter is to keep engaging with one another in exploring these issues. We cannot solve these issues by isolating them or pretending that they don't happen.

_____

_____

_____

_____

_____

_____

CHAPTER 14

MODEL OF DIVERSITY AND INCLUSION THAT IS HOLISTIC

As our world grows more complex, so does the complex nature of issues with diverse perspectives driven by multiple and dynamic experiences. These varied experiences provide the windows into the formulation of different perspectives. From the vantage of various lenses driven by a variety of experiences, I realized that given the nature of our global and institutional problems, thinking and acting alone in an effort to solve problems using a one-story narrative never works. It never works because of the limitations posed by the simple one-story narrative that does not include issues in their complicated forms. It simply does not work because such a simple-minded approach does not factor in sets of multiple-story narratives in a complex problem.

Our problems are too complex and therefore a simple one-story narrative, driven by one perspective, is insufficient in understanding multiple issues as necessary to get a grasp of the magnitude of different lenses through which the issues could be conceptualized and therefore does not provide sufficient resources to solve complex problems. Simply put, a one-story narrative or sound bite cannot be sufficient to solve complex and multiple dimensional stories driven problems. In order to effectively solve complex problems, we must begin to learn about the multiple-story narratives' associated problems that are often simplified by some to score points through one-liner catchphrases usually short in substance tailored for TV shows but rarely provide desired answers. The story narratives that are often bundled into a very narrow solution transmitted as solution does not work. It does not work because it doesn't provide for the depth and breadth of the complex issues necessary to answers the queries behind them, such as racial and gender identities that continue to present us with all kind of challenges, which we are not close to solving as evidence in our quest for racial and gender issues of our time.

In this chapter, we will look at a number of examples of these complex issues that are often dealt with as if they are simple and one-story-driven, which may explain why we have not sufficiently solved those issues, especially those of race and gender as well as how we label successful and unsuccessful people without holistic evaluation of the issues associated with whatever the story line one conveniently chooses.

First, let's begin by looking at identity and how we identify people based on our simplified and single narrowly socially engineered construct of identity. With reference to identity, let's begin with a question: How do we identify ourselves and each other? We have historically used identity to create divisions in our society, such as the one-drop rule, a term used as a social and legal classification that was historically prominent in the United States during the 20th century. It essentially asserted that any person with one ancestor of sub-Saharan African ancestry is considered black (Negro in historical terms).[86] In fact, it was conventional for the government to use such a classification as a way to identify and box black people into classifications when comparing persons, and such classification I contend still drives conscious and unconscious bias towards people of African ancestry. Such classification has been extended to other classifications that government organizations and private companies use to identify and categorize people on the basis of race, white, Asian, Hispanic, sexual orientation, gay, lesbian, or other categories, including religious, etc. In those simplified socially engineered structures, those categorized boxes are often used to discriminate and stereotype people as we often see in

---

[86] Khanna, Nikki. ""If you're half black, you're just black": reflected appraisals and the persistence of the one-drop rule." *The Sociological Quarterly* 51, no. 1 (2010): 96-121.

our day-to-day criminal justice system, especially from the perspectives of research and victims of such categorization. Even some business organizations are still using those structured and fixed-box methods to categorize people into boxes that buttress discriminatory practices driven by biased decision makers. It is a process that often leads to decisions used by some to determine who gets what and who is not purely based on those cultivated biases on the basis of one's race or gender, including decisions on who got hired or promoted, even though those practices are illegal. Those who categorize and put people in socially engineered boxes have failed to understand the whole person and the ignorance associated with their simplification driven by a single-story narrative of an individual's identity.

Before we look at examples, let's explore the issues in a personalized way with a question. Have you ever been subjected to a situation in which you were faced with having to claim half of who you are instead of the whole composition of who you are? Well, in a recent observation at the shopping center, I observed an African American woman with her two young children, a boy and a girl. As they waited for their turn so that the cashier could check them out with their purchases, a friendly customer service representative approached them and started speaking and complimenting them while I watched. It was an interesting conversation. The customer service person smiled, and these children reciprocated, obviously willing to speak with the store's customer service representative. The customer service person said to the children, "How are you?" The children opened up, and before the customer service representative could finish her statement, the girl asked her what's your name and where are you from? The salesperson responded, "I am from Canada." There was a pause that could be characterized as a surprise. Then the salesperson asked them, "Where are you guys from?" The boy responded, "I am from two countries, Ghana and Sierra Leone." He proceeded to explain further, "My dad is from Ghana and my mom is from Sierra Leone." The salesperson concluded, "You have got two of the best worlds." And they all laughed. These children were clearly proud of who they are, as was evidenced in the optimism with which they responded to those exchanges. The level of optimism experienced by children is often stolen from some people whose wholeness is often denied and forced into boxes our social structure created and boxed them in, as will be evidenced in the next scenario.

Contrary to the above situation, and in a different situation, a light-skinned girl who happened to be, according to one-drop rule characterization, classified as an African American child, had all kinds of ways she could describe herself, but there's only one way that she gets to be defined – a black girl who is light in complexion, according to the one-drop rule. A rule that denies the girl from the true composition of who she is.

Well, the reality is that here is a girl who could claim to be white, Irish, African, Chinese, and yes, a mixed child, and yet she would be looked upon as out of her mind if she claimed her fullness as the two previous children confidently and proudly claim their heritages and their historical roots. In this case, the girl's full wholeness is ignored; she is all that and I will illustrate in a moment. This is a girl whose grandparents on her maternal side are Irish American and Hispanic. On her maternal side, her father is an African American and mother a Jewish woman. She is combination of Jewish, African American, Hispanic, and God knows what else, but the question becomes *Why would the society continuously force her to choose to be less than 20 percent of what makes her?* Just because of our society's position of simplifying who she is because of our society's fixed mind set of classifying people, putting victims into boxes and yet lie or deny people being who they are because of TV simple-minded story narrative, and yet lie or deny it.

Now, consider yourself embodying something more than what the society boxes that often come into a number of categories. Categories in which people are asked to choose from and are often reflected in applications, government forms inform of questions, such as what's your race?

- ○ Box A. Black
- ○ Box B. White
- ○ Box C. Latino

Assume that you are like the young lady whose whole person comprises different backgrounds.

If you are all of the above but in a society where you are not recognized as consisting of all, and rather, people trying to tell you what you are on an ongoing basis, how would you feel?

As you go back to the earlier scenarios the girl that claimed to be from both Ghana and Sierra Leone, could you claim those without being worried? However, the girl who claimed all the components of her would be looked up on with disbelief because she looks mixed but in a society where she is looked upon to be 20 percent of what she is while being forced to drop 80 percent of who she actually is, that's what we are uncovering through the study of inter-sectionalism in race and ethnicity.

Most people think only about what they see and not the part from the other or the issues they neither could see nor understand when it comes to inter-sectionalism of issues. But such people have never considered the fact that one could be forced to choose who they are. However, if one goes back in history, perhaps during the time we would all like to forget or not remember, when people for convenience avoided who they were and rather passed for being white while some people were denied claiming that they were both black and white. Those who could pass for white consistently passed because it was easier and it availed them from going through the anguish and suffering the society could subject them to for being black or being suspected of being black. Now we are seeing the same with the advent of Artificial Intelligence, where bias on basis of race or gender among others continues to be ubiquitous in our society. This may sound strange, but consider these two identical story narratives by name.

Assume that a professional woman by the name of Bridget has grandparents who are white, African Americans, and Asians all combined in her paternal side of her family. And on her maternal side, her grandparents are a combination of Italian, Irish, and Hispanic. Based on our simplified model of Identity, Bridget may be asked and in fact is expected to fill any of the conventional boxes that forces her to check a box. What is she supposed to do? Check White, African American, Asian, Irish, or Hispanic? Bridget, of course, does not believe in those simplified boxes; she loves her whole identity and wants every one of her identities recognized and respected because they all combined to form her identity. Isn't it time for people to ban this simplified model of identity and bring the idea of whole personal identity, the one that includes that she is white, African American, Asian, Irish, and Hispanic? The answer calls for a full representation of one's identity, one that reflects all the beauty of who Bridget actually is instead of the simplified imposed false version of identity. Bridget's courage should be modelled by all of us, one that reflects the whole person's culture, ethnicity etc.

Secondly, there is the issue of poor or rich and stereotypes of poor and rich. Some people believe that whether one is rich or poor is driven by the individual's choice. On one hand, there is the popular notion that dictates if you are rich, it's because of your hard work, and on the contrary, if you are poor, it is because you are lazy. In this binary perspective, those who have cultivated such a belief fail to see the issues in context of their complexity because of their simplified narratives of rich versus poor. This simplistic model of conceptualizing complex issues does not provide us the answer for our complex and complicated problems as to why some people are rich and others are poor. To explore the complex nature of the issues of rich or poor, let me create four scenarios to demonstrate that whether one is rich or poor is not necessarily easily explained in a simplistic manner. We must begin to see and describe the complex issues that are associated with one's status in society.

Let's take John, for example. John is the son of two parents who struggled to get a good education from a fairly middle-of-the-road state university and not a big name school like Harvard, Yale, or the University of Chicago. Yes, John has earned a bachelor of science and an MBA in marketing. Well, because of John's limitation of infrastructural network, he did not get a big Wall Street job that some people get simply by their connection to big-name schools such as the ones listed above and he does not have people in top corporate and government positions to help connect him to big organizations where his talent could lead him to success. John's limitations to getting the job he is, of course, well-qualified for, as we have seen, could be constrained by where he went to school and his network infrastructure, and since he has neither, those could impede his ability to achieve the economic success someone else with a similar profile with the exception of either a big-name school or super infrastructural network of people who could not only introduce them to big corporate leaders via their connections, but could be helped by the guidance of the company in his community that is not like John's in terms of the environment that drives and determines success. These complex issues that are often associated with someone climbing the ladder, rich or poor, could be even more complicated than those expressed above. So the attempt by some to simplify complex issues and employ a simplistic model is simply insufficient to solving such problems.

Now, let's look at another aspect of our hollow evaluation and misconception of who makes it versus who does not. In this case, again, two people, one from a well-educated family that values education and believes that education would be the best thing they could provide their children above everything. The second person is a student, and let's call him Richard, from a very poor family, someone whose parents did not even finish high school. In this case, a teacher picked up interest in helping Richard. As result of the teacher's care, Richard succeeded with the help of his teacher. Richard learned so much that he was easily perceived as having a well thought-out plan and joy of education.

Clearly, in order to solve the complex issues associated with whether one is poor or rich, we have to look at the whole person and the entire and unique circumstances that factored the individual's becoming rich or poor. Those who are often quick to label people rich or poor must consider the various factors that drive one to be rich or poor, especially policymakers, who must abandon old and simple one-story narratives for a more complex approach, one that reflects the various complex issues as in the case of Richard. In Richard's case, in spite of being born and raised in a poor family, the teacher who became interested in him, his education, and his life circumstances helped Richard achieve in every aspect of life, including being rich. This is the part of the complex stories that the usual one single story does not include when snappy judgments of who is rich or poor are made. They conveniently exclude those complex issues associated with an individual's life circumstances.

A new paradigm that factors complex analysis and employs the whole gambits to make productive decisions as to the factors that foster whether one is rich or poor would include those unique circumstances such as those that have been revealed by Richard's teacher's intervention which can also be explain by the life cycle diagram below.

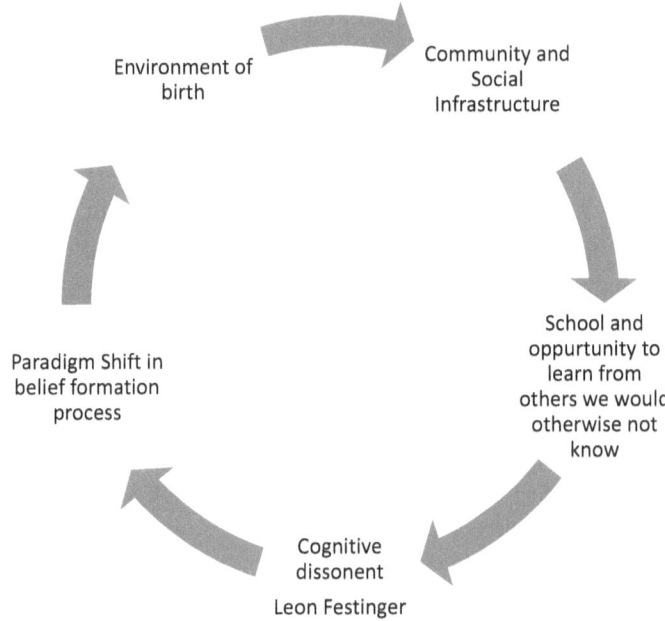

This model of holistic approach encompasses complex factors that will be revealed upon engaging with different people, whether it's those whose identities have been boxed to fit a mindset narrative of the poor, people who are often blamed for being poor, while the rich, lazy ones are characterized as rich and hard working.

Over the course of my work and experience, I realized that given the nature of our global and institutional problems, and the process through which we determine who is who, using a simplified model of thinking and acting using one-story narrative regardless of one's location in life continuum is no longer adequate. Our problems are too complex, and therefore, a simple one-story narrative will never provide the solutions we need for multiple-story narratives bound in one. Ladies and gentlemen, that is why I have always worked and to this day continue to work with diverse groups, groups with multiples narratives, multiple lenses that cumulatively provide enriched perspectives, and those have enormously informed and enriched me. Through those diverse groups such as the ones that are represented by these excellent panelists that shared their thoughts recently.[87] Through that process, I learned so much that I cannot possibly capture in words. However, I know that through open and honest engagement exploring various multiple-story narratives and collaborating with people, especially with those whose views and thoughts are different from mine and actively listening and engaging with them in debate and coordinating purposefully driven action plans in our common quest for equity and social justice for all, that experience has inspired me to do even more on the power of multiple stories to inform us as well and guide us on the power of a comprehensive approach to problem solving. To that end, whether you were in that wonderful and extraordinary panel discussion or you could not get in, I urge you to join us in a new paradigm of unity among all people to engage with each other in our effort to foster human-to-human connections driven by open and honest engagement with the aim of gaining an understanding of our complex issue of isms and helping one another to understand it in its complicated form in order to design an appropriate plan to solving them. The approach has inspired me to do more and I believe it will inspire you to do same through our Systemic Diversity and Inclusion Group. I want everyone to know that this is a forum where members can develop a sense of belonging and sharing ideas that buttress the human-to-human connection, but also provide members a forum for testing their hypotheses on issues associated with diversity and inclusion through meaningful engagement in ways that inspire them to collaborate with one another and ultimately form a united front in our collective efforts to create a better work environment, a better society where equity and social justice for all becomes the norm rather than the exception.

As we have seen in the above illustrations, we can understand the power of multiples narratives as they provide more and enriched perspectives.

---

[87] Nwoye, Joseph. 2019. Systemic Diversity and Inclusion Group Presents Her First Panel of Exceptional Professionals on Diversity and Inclusion. LinkedIn. https://www.linkedin.com/pulse/systemic-diversity-inclusion-group-presents-her-first-nwoye-ed-d-/

Clearly, as we can see, multiple narratives provide us more and enhanced opportunities for solving complex problems that simple single-narratives do not.

In terms of engaging in factors that are necessary for meaningful decisions, there are clearly so many challenges that one has to factor into it, and sometimes it involves complex issues that those who employ simple one-story narratives are either unaware of or deceptively avoid and neither is good because it often propels false narratives to prevail. People, especially those in leadership roles, must strive to find ways to move beyond simple one-story narratives and to become the kind of leader who is a strategic leader because they're looking at long-term goals and including what one-story narratives often exclude. In order to be that kind of leader, you have to really think about the world around you, the people around you, and yourself in new ways, and begin to see people in their various complex forms rather than boxing them up in the existing socially engineered simple boxes.

REFLECTION ON THE CHAPTER

As you finish reading the chapter, please reflect on how it resonates with you in the context of your past, present, and how the future looks. Please consider the past and your present experience as you proceed. As you think through those experiences, be specific as to how the chapter relates to your unique experience. Try to connect some of what you read to your own experience or the experience of other people that you know.

_____

_____

_____

_____

_____

_____

If you were able to relate or make connections, based on those connections you made, in what ways would you relay such powerful information to provide learning opportunities to others, especially young people?

_____

_____

_____

_____

_____

_____

In what ways has the content of this chapter helped you to ignite your metacognition while linking those experiences to multitudes of other experiences? As you reflect, please discuss how your experiences help foster meaningful understanding of the issues from one or more perspectives.

_____

_____

_____

_____

_____

_____

If you have no relatable experience, please feel free to express that too. The aim of this chapter is to keep engaging with one another in exploring these issues. We cannot solve these issues by isolating them or pretending that they don't happen.

_____

_____

_____

_____

_____

_____

CHAPTER 15

CONCLUSION

ERADICATING THE BIG ARTIFICIAL WALLS: BRIDGING THE DIVIDE TO PERFECT THE UNION

Beginning from the first chapter to this point, I wanted to ensure that two concepts are made crystal clear in a very concise manner. In fact, because these two concepts are essential for meaningful diversity and an inclusive community, where equity and social justice for all is not only spoken about, but more importantly, can be operational and all members of the community see the act of equity and social justice for all in practice. These two important concepts are belief formation and belief transformation. These concepts provide the conceptual framework for understanding how one's belief system informs his or her behavior – good or bad.

The concept-belief transformation provides the conceptual framework through which one can understand the process of belief transformation and how it influences change in human behaviors. The two concepts further enable us to learn and understand how our environment and issues we experience in life cumulatively shape our perception of reality and ultimately drive our behaviors. Clearly, people's belief systems and subsequent behavior explains why different people may look at one thing but have different views about it. Furthermore, it helps us to see and understand the issues that divide us and why. Divisions that help to explain the concept of "we versus them" for which we fight one another, discriminate against one another, and in some cases, kill one another. In this concluding chapter, I will reflect on brief historical and cultural issues that are pertinent to human behavior with a focus on belief formation and transformation that ultimately provides information on what drives human behavior, which I will get to in a moment, but before I get to that, let me reflect on a contemporary piece and how it aligns to the historical and cultural factors that influence historical and contemporary divides in our society and then proceed to providing strategies for bridging these historical, racial, cultural, and contemporary divides as evidenced throughout the book.

In recent article in the *Washington Post* (Dec. 25, 2017), titled "Bridging the divide: for Christmas…," the writer asserts, "The American house stands divided. In politics, at work, even in matters of love, we're constantly told that there is more tension than togetherness, that suspicion has prevailed over trust." The piece, in some ways, aligns with Woodard's assertion about American historical and cultural factors that explain our divisions.

Now that we have seen the similarity between the divisions illustrated by Woodard and the contemporary illustration of the existing divisions in our society, we will employ the highlights in the first chapters to further explore the historical and contemporary divisions in our society, and to also dive into the belief formation system and belief transformation, which cumulatively provided the framework for the entire book and certainly could be used as a guide for not only understanding, but provide the guideline for transformation that will provide the essentials for bridging our numerous divides.

In the first chapter, we laid out the historical foundations of our divisions and extent to which we are separated by our unique cultures that cumulatively influence varied belief systems; and thus, provide contexts for the positions we take on issues locally and in our larger community. These cultural differences and the degree to which we see things differently can be explained by the relative historical and cultural divisions in our society. Unfortunately, these divisions continue to exist, and we can't really address them without first accepting the fact that they exist. Denial or pretending that they do not exist, as some do, will not remedy the situation. We therefore must be united in accepting that there are divisions, and perhaps study the root causes that fostered the creation of those divisions in the first place and then put it in context.

In order to tackle our divisions, or issues that divide us, we must first accept that those divisions are real, and it's fitting here to reflect on President Abraham Lincoln's powerful words and reminder that these divisions must be eradicated when he stated, "A house divided against itself cannot stand." Clearly, despite President Lincoln's powerful reminder, we are still a house divided, and the reasons for these divisions are evidenced in our historical, geographical, cultural, racial, religious, and political backgrounds. In order to prevent these divisions, we must choose to confront the issues that divide us front and center and ensure that all these divisions are eradicated from our society.

President Lincoln's point about a house divided mirrors what we are experiencing in contemporary times. In closing, we will explore the factors that have and continue to influence the divisions in our society.

In order to narrow these divisions, we must adapt a new paradigm, one that calls for meaningful engagements on all fronts with the purpose of getting people to learn about one another and thus enable people to gain a good understanding of the issues and ultimately work to bridge the gap. This envisioned strategy would foster meaningful engaging debates in which opposing sides can debate issues and ultimately devise means that would ensure that those divisions come to an end, or at minimum, are reduced as much as possible.

For instance, debates between individuals, black and white, races, debates between MSNBC and Fox News representatives are not cocooned in information that reinforces their biases. To ensure that people are exposed to multiple perspectives, we must harness opportunities to allow various perspectives.

As shown in what Woodard characterizes as a time of "little mixing in their settlement streams," as politics, religion, ethnic prejudice, geography, and agricultural practices kept colonists almost entirely apart, we argue that although we mix with one another more than before, but still not sufficiently, otherwise, we would not be experiencing the differential treatment in almost all aspects of our lives as demonstrated in each of the chapters from the first to the last as summarized below:

In Chapter Two, we looked at the concept of the belief formation process with emphasis that our belief system is a function of our behavior. Regardless of what people say about their beliefs, whether they authentically and truthfully own it or deny it, they cannot divorce it from their behavior as illustrated in each chapter.

In Chapter Two, we dived into the belief formation process, but before we got to that, we posed some fundamental questions that would help every reader to understand how one's belief system is the function of the individual's behavior. Some of the questions read as follows:

What is it in our world that cultivates and shapes our belief system?

How does our belief system inform our conception of things?

How does our conception of things propel us to do what we do?

I encourage readers to keep those questions in mind and introspectively ask themselves these questions as well as others, because the answers to those questions are vital to understanding what informs almost all behaviors. Clearly, the exploration of those questions enables us to gain a deeper and better understanding as to why people do what they do regardless of whether they share our perspective on issues, and that would add value to our democratic process and foster meaningful debate on various issues.

In Chapter Three, we reflected on misconceptions that by and large usually stem from one's belief system. As we stated, our beliefs are a function of our behavior and our behavior reflects our experience. We looked at various misconceptions we may have been groomed with from childhood, and in some cases, compelled us to behave the way we do. As we evolve as human beings, we begin to gather new and more authentic information that compels us to see things from different lenses and thus change or transform our belief system. This in turn ushers in a new paradigm or modifies our way of seeing and interpreting things as exemplified in the earlier illustration with Santa Claus. As one grows up, he or she begins to see things with his or her naked eyes. Our new perspectives cumulatively propel us to question the earlier conception of things that are not in sync with our old belief system, and thus, we embrace a new perspective. As a result of this new authentic experience-based information, we are compelled to change or transform our beliefs.

As humans, we are social beings and our belief systems are formed by experiences through the company we keep. Paramount in the formation of our belief systems are shared history, ideas, values, and culture along with the values shared by family and peers. Take for instance in the United States, what happens when a Christian child is introduced to Santa Claus in a social environment where the child learns and develops a belief system that drives his or her perception of Santa Claus. Clearly, the child's introduction to Santa is shaped by the child's experience with Santa and the company one keeps helps in shaping one's belief system in the context of how he or she perceives the meaning of Santa Claus. If you were born and nurtured in the United States, you were probably eased into believing in Santa Claus. You were perhaps convinced to believe in the power of Santa Claus and his ability to shower you with great presents. The influence of peers and beloved ones in shaping behavior is evidenced too during Christmas time on how loved ones lead children to believe, especially when they come from the people they trust, their view may or may not necessarily be true, but it is just what one is prone to believe at a particular point in time from people one trusts, believes in, and loves. This kind of belief stays with the child as he or she grows up and learns. Upon learning and suddenly realizing that there is no such person as Santa Claus getting you presents as you were led to believe by those you love, trust, and believe in, you believed in what they taught you until your adult experience informed you differently, and as a result, you transformed your belief in Santa Claus to a more authentic one.

The above two chapters provided the foundations and the framework for understanding human behavior regardless of where an individual may come from or ideologies that may be driving the individual's behavior, and thus prepare you to be able to shift your cultural intelligence to deal with all human beings in a meaningful way.

REFLECTION ON THE CHAPTER

As you finish reading the chapter, please reflect on how it resonates with you in context of your past, present and how the future looks. Please consider the past and your present experience as you proceed. As you think through those experiences, be specific as to how the chapter relates to your unique experience Try to connect some of what you read to your own experience or the experience of other people that you know.

_____

_____

_____

_____

_____

_____

If you were able to relate or make connections, based on those connections you made. In what ways would you relay such powerful information to provide learning opportunities to others especially young people?

_____

_____

_____

_____

_____

_____

In what ways has the content of this chapter helped you to ignite your metacognition while linking those experiences to multitudes of other experiences? As you reflect, please discuss how your experiences help foster meaningful understanding of the issues from one or more perspectives?

_____

_____

_____

_____

_____

_____

If you have no relatable experience, please feel free to express that too. The aim of this chapter is to keep engaging with one another in exploring these issues. We cannot solve these issues by isolating them or pretending that they don't happen.

_____

_____

_____

_____

_____

_____

Thank you for reading,

Joseph Nwoye

"Dr. Nwoye has written an insightful and extremely relevant book for our times, that addresses the "grey" areas and helps us make sense of what is true and ethical. Joseph is not writing from theory, this book comes from his personal experiences and reflects his personal journey. If you are interested in diversity in education and in our society, you should read this book". **Dr. Mark D. DeHainaut, Cal U. (ret.)**

"Joseph shows us how to understand our belief systems and overcome cultural misconceptions while maintaining our humanity and optimism. His life's journey from Africa to America and his teaching experience at universities and with inner cities make his transformational strategies broadly applicable". **Deborah Levine, Editor-in-Chief. www. AmericanDiversityReport.com**

"Cultivating a belief system for peace, equity and social justice for all," provides us with an effective road map for addressing the complex issues of our time, especially those that divide us and continuously sap our ability to listen and understand one another. Above all, Dr. Nwoye's book equips us with the tools to engage and honestly address the issues of inequity while fostering harmony and peace for all".

Dr. Godson Chukwuma, Webster University.

"This book is the gift that Joseph was meant to give the world. The foundation of his views - a confluence of his travels, his extroverted personality and his unshakeable belief in people has opened his heart and given him the persistence to stay the course, until this moment. This book not only offers beautiful stories that people can use to learn more about why our differences matter and teach others to do the same, it will also enable communities to understand more about systemic changes that that could knock down the walls between us". **Pam Teagarden, MAPP, Partner with new AI models of "Inclusive Diversity."**

"Dr. Nwoye's thorough and incisive analysis of the belief formation process provides a useful lens to honor similarities and celebrate differences across cultural minefields. When we challenge unconscious past beliefs in light of the need to support our human family as much as our tribe, meaningful understanding becomes meaningful engagement becomes meaningful systems change. This book connects those dots".

Dr. Wayne Benenson.

www.ingramcontent.com/pod-product-compliance
Lightning Source LLC
Chambersburg PA
CBHW030921180526
45163CB00002B/425